From The Line In The Sand

Accounts of USAF Company Grade Officers in Support of Desert Shield/Desert Storm

edited by

Michael P. Vriesenga, Capt, USAF
Squadron Officer School

Air University Press
401 Chennault Circle
Maxwell AFB, Alabama 36112-6428

March 1994

Library of Congress Cataloging-in-Publication Data

From the line in the sand : accounts of USAF company grade officers in support of Desert
    Shield/Desert Storm / edited by Michael P. Vriesenga.
        p.   cm.
    Includes index.
        1. Persian Gulf War, 1991—Aerial operations, American.   2. Persian Gulf War, 1991—
    Personal narratives.   3. United States. Air Force—History—Persian Gulf War, 1991.
    I. Vriesenga, Michael P., 1957–
    DS79.724.U6F735   1994   94–1322
    959.7044'248—dc20   CIP

Disclaimer

This publication was produced in the Department of Defense school environment in the interest of
academic freedom and the advancement of national defense-related concepts. The views expressed
in this publication are those of the authors and do not reflect the official policy or position of the
Department of Defense or the United States government.

This publication has been reviewed by security and policy review authorities and is cleared for public
release.

For Sale by the Superintendent of Documents
US Government Printing Office
Washington, D.C. 20402

This book

is

dedicated to company grade officers,

past, present, and, especially, future.

Learn and grow!

Contents

RATED OFFICERS

ILLUSTRATIONS

PHOTOGRAPHS

Foreword

Helen Keller said: "The world is moved along, not only by the mighty shoves of its heroes, but also by the . . . pushes of each honest worker." As we look at history, we often limit our scope to the deeds and thoughts of those in command during times of crisis. In the case of DESERT STORM, accounts of the contributions of the great newsmakers are hitting the shelves with regularity. Harder to find are the perspectives of the many who contributed their individual pushes to the war effort. This book helps fill that void. It focuses on the contributions of company grade Air Force officers to victory in the desert.

The personal experiences presented here come from the heart of America's fighting force. They are but a few of the thousands of stories produced by the war. Some contain a bit of humor. Some are deadly serious. All are interesting and revealing. They reflect the continuing commitment and capability of America's military to protect and defend US interests. They also reflect the pride and individual skill of the men and women who comprise the world's finest fighting force.

Today's United States Air Force is one of the most complex of human endeavors—many thousands of people working together in hundreds of different specialties to defend America through control and exploitation of air and space. These specialties are interlocked and mutually supporting. This book may help you better understand how all that works as you read firsthand the experiences of the men and women who perform many of the specialties. In reading their stories, you'll also gain a better appreciation for the men and women themselves. They're real flesh and blood people who traveled a great distance to take on a very difficult task—and succeeded spectacularly. You'll experience their fear, frustration, fatigue, and boredom as well as their exhilaration and triumph.

What you glean from this book will depend on who you are, but I think there's something here of value for everyone—the experienced officer and the inexperienced, the military and the civilian. For us at Squadron Officer School, the book offers examples to help us in our mission of inspiring Air Force leaders of the future. We're grateful to Mike Vriesenga for conceiving the idea for the book, and for his considerable efforts in assembling it. We commend it to you.

JOHN W. BROOKS
Colonel, USAF
Commandant, Squadron
Officer School

About the Editor

Capt Michael P. Vriesenga

Capt Michael P. Vriesenga is force employment curriculum manager at Squadron Officer School, Air University, Maxwell Air Force Base (AFB), Alabama.

Captain Vriesenga was born on 4 November 1957, in Laredo, Texas, and graduated from Northeast High School in Fort Lauderdale, Florida, in 1975. He earned a bachelor of arts degree in history from Florida Atlantic University in 1980 and a master of arts degree in history from California State University at Sacramento in 1990. He was commissioned through OTS in 1982 and completed Squadron Officer School in 1989.

After completing navigator training, advanced navigator training, Survival School, and C-130 upgrade training, he was assigned to Little Rock AFB, Arkansas, as a C-130 navigator. Later, he volunteered to return to Mather AFB, California, as a DOD instructor navigator. While there, he created and produced the 50th anniversary edition of *The Navigator* magazine.

In 1990, he was assigned to the Squadron Officer School as a flight commander. After a year as a flight commander, he transferred to the Aerospace Division as the aerospace doctrine phase manager.

Captain Vriesenga is a senior navigator with over 2,000 flying and simulator hours. His military decorations and awards include the Air Force Commendation Medal with one oak leaf cluster,

National Defense Service Medal, Air Force Longevity Service Award, Marksmanship Ribbon, and Air Force Training Ribbon. He was promoted to captain in November of 1986. Captain Vriesenga is married to the former Vickie Lee Evans of Cincinnati, Ohio. They have one child: Patrick.

Acknowledgments

Clearly, this book would have been impossible without the sacrifice of time and effort of the individual authors. I would also like to acknowledge those authors who sent me stories which, for various reasons, are not published here. I have donated all the unedited stories to the USAF Historical Research Agency at Maxwell AFB.

The faculty at SOS was fundamental to creating this book. Gen Lance W. Lord supported this idea. His support opened the doors which took this from an idea to a project. I also appreciate my office mates at SOS/EDCD for helping to carry my weight and patiently allowing me to monopolize their computers while this was coming together. I hope that future faculty and students find the experiences included here valuable.

Thanks are due to Preston Bryant and many others at Air University Press for helping me get this composite essay published.

Finally, thanks to my wife, Vickie, for her unfailing prayers and enthusiasm for this project, despite the crosses she had to bear.

Introduction

This book is a compilation of autobiographical stories of captains and first lieutenants who contributed to the Gulf War. I first thought of trying to collect these stories in the fall of 1991. As a historian, I thought they would be valuable additions to the historical record. In that sense, I viewed this as a modified oral history—historical accounts as told by the participants. As an instructor at Squadron Officer School (SOS), I thought this would be a valuable teaching tool. I hoped future officers could pick this up and understand, from firsthand information, what it means to be a company grade officer at war. Hopefully, you can see here in concrete some of the abstract ideas from Air Force Pamphlet (AFP) 35-49, *Air Force Leadership,* and Air Force Manual (AFM) 1-1, *Basic Aerospace Doctrine of the United States Air Force.* Finally, I began assembling these stories out of a sense of fairness. You can walk into any library or bookstore and read about the Gulf War according to Norman Schwarzkopf. You can pick up contemporary news magazines and read about some of the heroes of the war. Until now, you would have to look long and hard to find out what it means to be a company grade officer in any war, including the Gulf War. In fact, I almost changed the name of the book. An office mate showed me Bob Woodward's *The Commanders,* about those who led the war. I considered naming this *The Operators,* based on Paul Johnson's term for the hands-on line officer. Although this is a colorful term, it's too narrow. Line officers are not just operators. They are thinkers, feelers, and leaders without whom the commanders would be ineffective and out of touch, and the enlisted would be lost. My fondest wish for this book is that it help to produce better company grade officers for future wars.

I pitched the idea to Brig Gen Lance W. Lord, commandant of SOS, who liked the idea well enough to send a letter to Air University Press. I explained the idea to a panel of people over at Air University Press, and they agreed to print what I produced.

The second step in putting this together was to solicit articles. General Lord signed letters to as many wing commanders as I could find from the Gulf War, asking them to encourage their folks to write. *Air Force Times, Air Force Magazine, Airpower Journal,* and *TAC Attack* were kind enough to advertise the project. Finally, I encouraged each class of SOS students to contribute to the project. Eventually, the articles trickled in. I read and edited each article before sending it off to Preston Bryant for more editing. Finally, the articles themselves were complete.

I struggled for some time over how to arrange the articles. Although I wanted to avoid perpetuating the rated/support dichotomy, I settled on that arrangement because it seemed understandable. I hope that you read all the articles, but particularly those that are outside your specialty or command. If there is any common thread between these articles, it is that the Air Force is a team and it takes all the players working together to be most effective. You might not take your teammates for granted if you better understand how they contribute to the team's success.

The article by Paul Johnson is an edited transcript of his presentation on stage at SOS. I think you will find Capt Moscarelli's article rich with the flavor of the war.

Although, or perhaps because, I am a navigator, I found the support articles fascinating and important. Ed O'Connell wrote the single most exciting "war story," and I think you will enjoy walking through the war in his shoes. Kennedy, Smith, and Scardera bring out aspects of the war that you probably didn't know about and should. Koehler and Folmar wrote articles that are both fun and interesting.

I hope you find value in all the articles and I hope you can benefit personally and professionally from their stories and examples. I hope you gain from this book a deeper understanding of the Air Force and its officership.

SUPPORT OFFICERS

Men of the Stratofortress

by

Capt Michael D. Madzuma*
1st Lt Michael A. Buoniconti*

Strategic Air Command's (SAC) B-52G bomber, aged though it is, remains the most formidable manned weapon system in the Air Force inventory. A sledgehammer on continuous alert to smash America's most threatening foe with nuclear weapons, yet the B-52G is also prepared to crush a lesser foe with nearly 20 tons of conventional munitions. B-52 aircrews made the awesome weapons system capable of executing nuclear or conventional missions.

Beginning in August 1990, B-52G aircrews proved that capability—maintaining nuclear deterrence while preparing for, and finally executing, the conventional thunder of Operation Desert Storm. Wurtsmith Air Force Base's (AFB) aircrews were among those who answered the call. This is the story, from the perspective of two non-flying staff officers who helped prepare those aircrews for combat.

Seeds of Involvement

Initial US military deployments to Saudi Arabia (August 1990) sparked little more than professional curiosity within SAC's 379th Bombardment Wing (BMW) at Wurtsmith AFB. It was clearly a Tactical Air Command show—a defensive operation, with Langley AFB's F-15 fighters as the vanguard. Wurtsmith's B-52Gs continued to pull 24-hour alert, maintaining nuclear deterrence. Life appeared unaffected by events in the Persian Gulf.

*The authors wish to thank Ms Susan Webb for her preliminary editing work on this article.

1

Over the following four months, the tempo of wing preparations (for potential deployment to the Gulf) quickened. By November, an advance echelon from the 379th BMW was established at Jedda, Saudi Arabia, preparing the way for a full deployment.

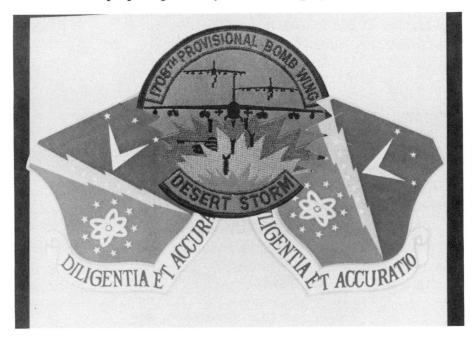

1708th Provisional Bomb Wing

The intermittent trickle of personnel to Jedda became a full flow in late December as the 379th BMW became the lead element of what would be the 1708th Provisional Bombardment Wing (PBW). Deployment surprised those affected. Perhaps the ever-changing rosters of potential "deployees" in the months prior had lent an air of unreality to the whole affair. Or perhaps it was because life at Wurtsmith remained unchanged. The *existing* mission of deterrence continued as normal, with B-52Gs poised on round-the-clock alert. Home-front preparations for the *potential* conventional mission in the Gulf, however intense, remained behind the scenes.

In Jedda, Wurtsmith staff officers comprised the provisional wing's operations planning team (OPT). These staff officers faced a formidable challenge as augmentees arrived from different B-52G units. They had to convince each new crew member that the provisional wing's concept of operations was sound and that aircrew interests were foremost in the mind of each OPT member. Credibility was at stake. SAC aircrews, who for years had planned their own missions and mastered low-altitude penetration, would now fly OPT-planned missions at high altitude. This new concept was clearly at odds with SAC bomber culture, which had evolved from perceived problems in Vietnam two decades earlier. To make matters worse, the bearers of this 1708th PBW heresy were Wurtsmith staff officers, strangers to most augmentee crew members.

Fortunately for the OPT, Wurtsmith aircrews had arrived with a general knowledge of the Iraqi threat environment, which drove the wing's concept of operations. Their insights, during off-duty conversations with skeptical peers, helped overcome augmentee resistance. Lingering doubts were not entirely erased until seriously battle-damaged aircraft from other units recovered at Jedda after the first day's low-level strikes.

Though launched throughout the Gulf, Operation Desert Storm did not emanate from Jedda on 17 January 1991. The wing was fully prepared, but no B-52Gs were yet deployed. The highlight of that night, since intelligence message traffic was already behind the rush of events, was OPT debriefings of several F-111 aircrews who

Old Crow Express

recovered at Jedda. But this bit of secondhand combat news brought little release to a charged-up 1708th PBW.

Off to War

"Their faces . . . the aircrews just don't seem to realize that they are about to go to war . . . that this is the real deal."

In fact, it was truly difficult to comprehend what the 10 Wurtsmith B-52Gs, which had taken off only minutes prior, were about to do. In about 14 hours, on 18 January 1991, these B-52Gs would drop *real* bombs on *real* people almost half the world away. An awesome feat—to launch bombers from Michigan, aerial refuel them twice, bomb the Republican Guard in Iraq, and finally land in Saudi Arabia. At 379th BMW, this mission was referred to simply as "The Employ/ Deploy," a mission which would introduce Wurtsmith's B-52Gs to the Iraqis much like a wrecking ball to a glass house.

As Employ/Deploy approached, the usually hollow halls behind the secure "Green Door" of Intelligence became gridlocked with aircrews scrambling for the latest scoop on the crisis. Intelligence message traffic, which normally became nothing more than a fine ornamental piece in our vault decor, was actually read by the aircrews. We no longer needed trivia questions to capture aircrew attention (even tanker crews). This had to be real.

Indeed, it was real. As this reality set in, internal bickering amongst the aircrews became somewhat heated. In spite of significant expected losses, most aircrews wanted to go. Those who were not selected to deploy were generally resentful. However, because Wurtsmith was still tasked with nuclear deterrence, some had to stay and sit alert. While frustration levels were rising, final preparations for the Employ/Deploy were being completed.

Following the pretakeoff briefing, mission planners wished the aircrews well and gave them soda and snacks as a gesture of moral support. Understandably, many of the crew members had no appetite for food and, as on any occasion, a few self-serving opportunists took full advantage of the situation. As emotional stress was reaching a feverish pitch, these "crewdogs" filled their flight suits to the bursting point with goodies.

Members of the combat intelligence shop lingered well past midnight at 379th BMW headquarters and watched the B-52Gs launch into the ironically peaceful sky. In a matter of hours, the bombers' rage would dramatically strengthen the fury of Desert Storm.

Toil in the Gulf

None of the 18 crew members present for the first 1708th PBW strike briefing squirmed in their seats. In fact, it seemed no one so much as blinked an eye during the entire 30 minutes. Attention was absolutely focused on the tactical planning chart displayed at the front of the room with route and target annotated. The threat rings . . . lots of them . . . the wing commander . . . the chaplain reading from the Bible . . . this was real.

Meanwhile, the OPT was already working the next mission. We updated the threat rings, chose a minimum risk route, coordinated defense suppression and fighter support, and completed the other tasks required to present a completed package to three more aircrews three hours later. Each task was checked and cross-checked, but each OPT member still wondered if he could have done something more or something better for the previous mission. Perhaps a more thorough strike briefing with a little threat/tactics review? No. The director of operations had already settled that issue. For the aircrews, "school" was out; it was time to apply those years of training. "Shorter is better" governed strike briefings, leaving maximum time for crew study. Crew members would ask for more information if they needed it.

The next strike briefing went much the same. Three hours later, we did another one: Around-the-clock production for the OPT, with each mission package crafted to be as route-specific and threat-current as possible for its strike briefing. Another call to ensure F-4G Wild

Weasel and F-15 support . . . a call to Central Air Forces (CENTAF) for a target area update 15 minutes before departure.

We were stressed because we had no bomb damage assessments (BDA) or poststrike photos. Without pictures, we didn't know whether the crews had put their bombs on the target. The crews asked for results, too. We called SAC or CENTAF, whatever it took, for BDA support.

Another strike briefing, another shift, another week! The atmosphere loosened, and it was spiced with sarcasm about the Iraqis. Confidence went extremely high since we had no losses and very little battle damage. The director of operations cautioned his crews about overconfidence, reminding them that they were not men of steel.

Aircrew morale was a challenging issue. The vast majority of missions were flown against Iraqi ground forces in the desert, and the few available poststrike photos showed only bomb craters in the sand—hardly a morale booster for those who risked it all. Under these circumstances, the OPT's ground liaison officer (GLO) assumed an importance far beyond his limited operational value during the air campaign. The GLO coaxed his ground operations contacts into speculating about the state of Iraqi units after B-52 strikes, and he briefed each mission on the latest twist in such speculation. He may have even exaggerated a little.

Stress! "What do you mean we can't get dedicated Weasel support? These B-52Gs are not exactly agile airplanes! What's the alternative? None available? Can't they do an area sweep beforehand? Okay, a Weasel sweep prior to time-over-target. Do it!"

Relaxation! What will I do during the three hours remaining until shift begins? I already slept a full eight hours. The surrounding area is off-limits due to the terrorist threat. I'll try the donated books again, but there were only romance novels last time. Should I write a couple of letters, lie around in the sun, jog a little, eat a full meal?

After Diego Garcia lost one B-52, though not from hostile fire, everyone was somber, especially during the next several strike briefings. The chaplain's briefings were a little longer. The DO no longer needed to caution the crews against overconfidence.

Stress! "How could there be so many threats if Weasels were launching hundreds of HARMs (high speed antiradiation missile)? Prove it, Intel! You can't prove it because you have no imagery backup for electronic intelligence. Okay then, let's penetrate that ring to minimize overall exposure in hostile airspace. No, we can't support that plan. Let's go around it. There's not enough maneuver room for a BUFF (B-52)? Okay, let's skirt the edge of the ring. Okay."

Excitement! Poststrike feedback for one of our aircrews reports the biggest nonnuclear explosion in modern warfare. There are smiles all around, but also a hint of envy. That lucky crew always got the good targets. They must have buddies working the air tasking order.

Flyers on OPT staff began to pressure anyone with influence over the flying schedule. All wanted the opportunity to fly combat missions, either as staff crews or as one-for-one replacements on existing combat crews. Senior staff members invoked their authority as arbiters of the flying schedule. Combat crews would *fly* missions and OPT staff would *plan* them, except in unusual situations.

Tension Builds on the Home Front

While Desert Storm raged in the Persian Gulf, a different anger swelled back at Wurtsmith. The aircrews, sitting on alert every other week, were growing more and more frustrated as reports of coalition bombing successes piled up. Though they lauded their peers' performance, the alert crews seemed to feel that their chance to fly even one combat mission was quickly slipping away. And without any combat experience, their post–Gulf War Air Force futures would be severely handicapped.

Consequently, even delivering intelligence briefings to the alert crews had become a form of hazardous duty. On one occasion, an aircraft commander (AC) relentlessly attacked the briefer over an inconsistency between his bomb damage report and that of a report by General Schwarzkopf on CNN. The briefer finally staved off the

AC's verbal attack by sharply suggesting that, if he must know, he was welcome to give the general a call and ask for an explanation himself. The standing ovation which that suggestion ignited shamed the AC into silence. Clearly, accepting the much less dramatic role of maintaining nuclear deterrence was very difficult for many.

Victory and Return

For B-52G aircrews of the 1708th PBW, Operation Desert Storm ended almost as suddenly as it had begun. The rapid victory on the ground, though planned as such, caught many by surprise. Combat crews began redeploying shortly after the cease-fire agreement. Those from Wurtsmith were folded into 379th BMW's alert force schedule as soon as possible. The final tally for 1708th Bomb Wing: 846 combat sorties that dropped over 25 million pounds of munitions (more than 20 percent of total coalition ordnance expended) in 42 days. Not a single aircraft was lost. For aircrews who remained at Wurtsmith, a less ballyhooed but no less complete victory would come in the waning hours of 1991: The official dissolution of the Soviet Union on 31 December 1991 would end the cold war.

Only the aircrews of the B-52G were called upon to fight two wars at one time. Their simultaneous contributions to victory in the Gulf War and the cold war is a unique achievement. The G-model's aircrews clearly demonstrated, abroad and at home, their dual-role capability. In their hands, the Stratofortress truly was a sledgehammer.

Wings over Britain:
A Model for Our Next War?

by

Capt Gregory J. Touhill

In Operation Desert Storm, the B-52 bomber flew high- and low-altitude missions against targets in Iraq and Kuwait from locations outside the area of responsibility (AOR). A minimally manned "caretaker" facility such as RAF Fairford may serve as an example for operations in the future and spur the restructuring of our foreign-based forces.

Background

The dissolution of the Warsaw Pact changed the European defense fabric. One result was that RAF Fairford was mothballed in 1990. The rationale was simple: with fewer aircraft flying in Europe, fewer refuelings were needed. The tanker force at RAF Mildenhall could meet the theater's needs. Fairford was drawn down rather than closed because it is a major communications node and because it has runways and taxiways that can support large, heavy aircraft. A small cadre of 50 Air Force personnel were selected to remain on site to maintain facilities, operate vital communications systems, and beddown aircraft during regular B-52 deployments.

The 7020th Air Base Squadron was formed (1 October 1990) to keep RAF Fairford an active, viable facility. I was the commander of the 2160th Communications Squadron, and I was asked to stay on as the 7020th Air Base Squadron deputy commander for a few months to supervise the 30 communications and air traffic controllers, oversee the transition of equipment, work airspace issues, and create plans for future beddowns. Little did I know that the plans I wrote would be executed in a few months.

Fairford Enters the War

Throughout Operation Desert Shield, USAFE and Third Air Force headquarters told us to be ready to receive aircraft. As a large airdrome, we were capable of receiving and turning bomber and airlift aircraft. Deployments of bombers to Moron Air Base, Spain, and to Diego Garcia portended a possible Fairford deployment, but no tasking materialized. Maintenance and transportation equipment stored at Fairford was quickly "reallocated" to higher priority sites while the caretaker staff maintained its high state of readiness. However, just when the war seemed to be "passing us by," we got our first tasking.

Lt Col Tom Graves, the base commander, received word that the 870th Contingency Hospital at RAF Little Rissington was being opened to handle possible war casualties. We would billet approximately 2,000 medical personnel at our facilities, so our small staff quickly became a services organization before the "experts" arrived. To supplement our dormitories and billeting facilities, Capt Jim Benson, our base civil engineer, and SSgt Roy Jackson, our lone services member, converted as many facilities as possible, including the school, to dormitories.

SSgt Bill Kenyon, our comm-computer systems programs manager, developed a billeting data base and ran the in-processing while Mr Russ House, our commercial communications manager, asked British Telecom to install pay telephones for the troops. Within days, we bedded 1,500 medical troops; then we tried to find enough activity to keep them occupied, since no casualties seemed to be headed our way.

As the United Nations deadline approached and war appeared imminent, I placed our communications center on 24-hour manning. I had only three people remaining from my original 15-member team, so Airmen Chris McIntire and Mike Dixon set up cots, sleeping bags, and a microwave oven in order to "live" in the comm center, which was serving as the base's command post. The war was barely into its second week when we learned we would receive the 806th Provisional Bomb Wing. As the communications commander, my responsibilities included air traffic control, command post, comm center, switchboard, computers, and radios. (If it had current running through it, I was responsible.) Fortunately, I had handpicked a motivated and capable caretaker staff during the drawdown. This made activating RAF Fairford easy. Unfortunately, my assignment technically ended in January, so Colonel Graves and I decided to postpone my departure while my family (and furniture) returned to the United States.

SMSgt Bob Russel, my chief of air traffic control, and I met with our British counterparts to arrange for B-52 airspace approaches and departures, coordinate emergency procedures, arrange for air traffic control briefings to the aircrews, and identify "pickling" areas for emergency bomb release. Our British allies at RAF Brize Norton were superb. Despite the tremendous air traffic load out of their own facility and RAF Upper Heyford, they worked extremely well with us to ensure that we had no late takeoffs and that we always had skies clear of commercial traffic.

Meanwhile, MSgt Ron Braley, my maintenance superintendent, and his staff double-checked all our communications, meteorological, and navigational aid equipment to ensure that they were ready for combat aircraft. Despite our drawdown status, our maintenance personnel continued to service and operate our system to support transitory aircraft and our continuing communications mission.

The base command post needed to be "reactivated," so we strung cable television into the area (for CNN) and installed an AN/UYK-83A AUTODIN terminal for status reporting. Sergeant Braley spent two nights installing the UYK-83A, which operated flawlessly during the remainder of the war. Simultaneously, Mr Al Quesnel, my telephone maintenance expert, and I coordinated with the Defense Communications Agency (DCA), Headquarters USAFE, and Headquarters SAC to support the bomber force. Although a normal circuit activation can take as much as a year to complete, we got next-day service. Much of the thanks for that goes to Mr Marco Voich, the Third Air Force circuit manager, who knows everyone in the business and gets things done.

Three days after we were notified, the 806th Provisional Bomb Wing, under Col George Conlan, arrived. Before the base drawdown,

I had commanded a squadron of 120 people. Now I had greater tasking, but only 30 people—30 people who had been working around-the-clock for two weeks. I called Col Jerry Reinholt, Third Air Force's 2147th Communications Wing commander, for help. Colonel Reinholt and his staff immediately sent more than 50 people, as well as computers and other equipment, to support the wing. Additionally, 2d Lt Alishia Holder and a combat crew communications team provided combat mission folders for the crews. Our team intact, we were ready as the wing began bombing.

Bedding down the wing was easy; the systems were already in place and ready to go. The complex communications and computer systems needed for the intelligence support mission were a challenge that my staff and I made our top priority. I met with Major Moore, the intelligence chief, and together we identified critical and secondary systems. I coordinated with DCA-Europe and British Telecom to install a circuit for the Defense Integrated Secure Network (DISNET) within hours. I worked with Colonel Reinholt to secure a computer system and technician from RAF Bentwaters to give the wing access to this worldwide intelligence network. I also brought a technician from RAF Upper Heyford to perform hands-on training with the 806th intelligence staff. We installed circuitry for the Digital Imagery Transmission System (DITS) to support targeting and bomb damage assessment. Although the unit was too big to fit through the doors to our vault, we put it in an adjacent room, reran the phone lines, and hooked up a 9,600-bit-per-second STU-III to facilitate data transfer. In addition to the DISNET and DITS, we installed 14 separate stand-alone intelligence computer systems, including SENTINEL BYTE and CONSTANT SOURCE, to support the intelligence effort.

Transporting bombs from RAF Whelford to RAF Fairford was a politically sensitive subject. Even though there was no genuine threat from terrorists or peace movement activists, we took special precautions. Working with the British Ministry of Defense, we established convoy routes and a cellular telephone network to keep the convoys in touch with command post, security, and local constabularies.

The cellular phones worked great for the convoys, but intra-base communication was a touchy subject. Before the drawdown, RAF

Fairford had what the USAFE inspector general team called "the best" land mobile road network in the command. Unfortunately, most of the systems had been deployed to the Gulf during Operation Desert Shield.

When I received notice of the 806th activation, I coordinated with the Headquarters SAC battle staff and reminded them that conventional stateside radios were outside our bandwidth. Radios needed to be in the British-approved frequencies. The wing arrived with factory-fresh Motorola Radius P-200 radios that were underpowered for the terrain around RAF Fairford. Maintenance troops couldn't communicate from one end of the two-mile-long runway to the other. This caused an intolerable situation for the deputy commander for maintenance, Col Tom Patterson, who told me to fix it.

After our Motorola contractor said he couldn't fix the problem, TSgt Bob Batsche and Sergeant Bill Kenyon set about making the system work. They developed a unique "tune-up" procedure for the radios that decreased the frequency shift by over 1,000 percent and boosted the output power by nearly 100 percent. Through their innovative use of computers and simple test equipment, and their own sense of urgency, they provided a critical link for maintenance personnel.

Another critical link on the ground was the Core Automated Maintenance System (CAMS). Eighth Air Force maintenance planners had projected a need for only eight CAMS terminals, but we actually needed over 20 terminals. We coordinated with RAF Upper Heyford to return much of the CAMS equipment we had distributed to them after our drawdown, worked with British Telecom to run new CAMS circuits to the needed locations, fabricated our own cables for installation, and trained the maintenance data base manager on the system. Despite the fact that we had an initial capability on line in two days, CAMS never lived up to its full potential because maintenance troops were located over a mile from where they were projected to be and where their preplanned circuits were already in place.

Security was critical to our operations. SSgt Gay Skinner arranged for over 300 pounds of codebooks, authentication tables, and other COMSEC materials to be delivered within hours of our initial tasking. We coordinated with the Defense Courier Service at RAF Mildenhall and with the Air Force Cryptological Support Center at Kelly AFB, Texas, to make sure we got the materials we needed. We were authorized local reproduction and had all necessary materials on hand for each mission.

Secure communication was critical, particularly for the command post. We had mothballed the command post by deleting as many expensive, dedicated circuits as we could and replacing them with computerized speed-dialed circuits. Connecting with Riyadh, Ramstein, and Offutt was never a problem since we had at least three circuit paths (voice, data, or satellite) constantly available. However, the wing commander wanted to be able to contact the planes in flight while they traveled to and from the area of responsibility. I happened to know where some war reserve materiel (WRM) PACER BOUNCE radios were, and I had some old high-frequency (HF) radio antennae available, so my radio troops hooked up a high-frequency radio for the wing command post.

The HF radio turned out to be invaluable one night during a bombing mission when one of our aircraft lost electrical power. Because they

A B-52 Laden with Bombs

Takeoff

Return Landing

were on batteries, the crew needed to ditch their bombs and find an emergency landing field. Moreover, their braking power was dicey without their primary electrical system. The command post gave constant instructions to the aircrew who, in order to save their power, did not respond. The aircraft commander decided to land at Palermo, Italy. I coordinated with Comiso Air Base and NATO's southern headquarters in Naples to secure the plane upon landing. Within 30 minutes of their emergency landing in Palermo, a US Marine Corps security team was guarding the aircraft. (Within one hour, they were on CNN.)

Another challenge involved an experiment with voice communications and a satellite transceiver. The B-52G is equipped with a data-only satellite terminal. Eighth Air Force loaned us a few LST-5B UHF satellite terminals for data, fax, and voice communications, and we decided to try to rig one into the aircraft. Sgt Andy Lethko, a wideband radio expert, worked with the flight-line maintenance troops while I coordinated with Colonel Patterson to ensure that we didn't violate any configuration control on the aircraft. We trained the gunner to switch between data and voice capability by connecting a coaxial cable to different ports. Although the system showed promise, the war ended before we fully developed it.

Much has been said about the computer-assisted force management system (CAFMS) and its ability to get the air tasking order (ATO) out to the field. However, CAFMS was trouble for us. Initially, CENTAF-Forward did not have the computer port availability for us; we received our ATO via AUTODIN. Since Sergeant Braley had just installed a semiautomated remote AUTODIN host (SARAH) terminal in the comm center with a modem and a high-speed printer, we were getting the ATO relatively quickly. CENTAF-Rear then directed us to get a computer, some crypto gear, and a computer program that we didn't have access to, in order to hook up to CAFMS. I managed to get the computer, but the crypto wasn't available in the United Kingdom— and I didn't have any computer programmers (or experienced operators) to work the CAFMS program. I arranged for a crypto unit and operator to initialize the system. Installed days before the shooting stopped, CAFMS did not impact our operations.

Aftermath

The 806th's mission concluded almost as fast as the wing had formed. Fairford troops accomplished a lot in a short period of time. They activated over 800 telephones and circuits, installed over 115 computers and a complete intelligence comm-computer system, negotiated air traffic control procedures, worked munition convoy issues, and bedded down a large contingency hospital and a bomb wing—all in a two-week period. With 30 communicators and air traffic controllers, we did more than most large communications squadrons do. Could the Air Force do this again?

Absolutely! In fact, in this age of diminishing resources, we need to consider, evaluate, and implement methods of multiplying our forces. By locating small teams of caretaker forces in strategic locations, we can make global reach more efficient, economical, and safe. Wings will be able to coordinate plans with air base squadrons ahead of time, and can practice deployments in a CHECKER-FLAG-type scenario. The cost of maintaining a full base may be avoided.

The composition of this base of the future is debatable. Because we must provide at least basic utilities, some civil engineering and communications specialists will be required. Because comm-computer systems are vital to the infrastructure of every organization in the wing, the comm-computer system team must be able to connect into the major communications and computer system nodes. Moreover, they must be able to work with host-nation communications providers to ensure host-nation connection and frequency allocation. Civil engineers are needed to maintain the basic infrastructure, although local national services can provide the bulk of facility operations and maintenance.

During Operation Desert Storm, RAF Fairford proved that a drawdown base can provide a quick-reaction air base with minimal personnel and maximum capability as our forces provide global power and global reach for America. Future strategists may find that a forward-deployed drawdown facility may be a cost-effective alternative for theater force employment.

Desert Storm Chapstick

by

Capt John T. Folmar

There I was . . . on the golf course at Randolph AFB, Texas. It was a Saturday in October 1990, much like any other early autumn week-end day. But a line had been drawn in the sand, and on this day US troops were pouring into the Gulf like fans through the turnstiles at a Braves game. But that was over there, and this was the heart of Air Training Command (ATC). Frankly, I had been more concerned with the fiscal year closeout than the massive deployment of soldiers and airmen.

In the distance, I could see the club pro approaching my group on the eighth green. His presence was usually reserved for matters of some urgency, but I never thought he was seeking me. "Ah, the good Lieutenant Folmar, just the man I am looking for. You have an emer-gency call in the clubhouse," he said. I gasped out loud. My wife knew better than to interrupt my weekend pastime. And why today, when I was only two over?

Reluctantly, I trudged in. The chief of supply was on the line, requesting my immediate presence at the command post. I didn't ask why a lowly base-level contracting officer was so directly needed— I forfeited the golf match and proceeded to the directed destination.

I soon discovered that, yes indeed, ATC was supporting this Desert Shield thing. In fact, dozens of 12th Flying Training Wing personnel were processing through the mobility line when I arrived. I still was not cognizant of what was going on, and I felt very much out of place. Dressed in golf togs, I was surrounded by pallets of A-3 bags and uniformed soldiers. I was quickly ushered aside and shown

19

what appeared to be a standard Air Force message. It contained a laundry list of mandatory mobilization items. Buried in the text was a one-liner that suddenly brought light to this clouded fog: "Local responsibilities of the augmenting units." With the clue bird now perched on my shoulder, I focused on items of peculiarity. "Sunscreen" and "chapstick" immediately caught my attention. These are standard gear for a beach trip, but they are not required to fight a war, are they? I tried to ascertain an appropriate course of action. Here we had young men and women, transportation, supply, security police, all sorts of folks and ranks, preparing to deploy to Saudi Arabia. Some looked excited, some looked scared. All I knew was they weren't going anywhere until they got some chapstick!

Instinct propelled me to the yellow pages, where I nervously trusted my shaking fingers to find a source of supply for 300 bottles of sunscreen and 300 tubes of chapstick. Drug stores, drug stores, I thought. Surely there was a warehouse in San Antonio just full of this stuff. After four phone calls, I found someone who would take me seriously, and they checked with the manager's manager to determine availability and pricing. Since this was not exactly the answer the chief of supply had in mind, I filled the time with idle chatter about procurement regulations and paperwork requirements. (I was trying to project an air of competency.)

After what was assuredly the longest 45 minutes of my life, my newfound good friends at a local drug store said they would scramble and empty their shelves to meet what I believed to be the most pressing and urgent requirement in the Air Force.

When I picked up the sundries, the local vendor said he was honored to contribute to the looming international crisis and would offer this truckload of desert sun protection at a discount of over 60 percent. Having orchestrated a deal that would make my Dad, if not Donald Trump, proud, I realized that within two hours of notification I had successfully executed an emergency contracting acquisition in support of what was one of the United States military's finest moments.

Trivial to be sure, but a Saturday morning effort I will not soon forget. Of me, they did not ask much. But it is with great pride that I serve, and it feels good to know that when the bell rang, I answered. No Air Medals for this boy, just an oft-used bullet statement that reads, "Negotiated the acquisition of critical and time-sensitive sundry supplies for deploying Air Force troops in support of Operation Desert Shield/Desert Storm."

Engineering from Rock to Sand

by

1st Lt Gregory S. Brown

Serving as a USAF civil engineering officer in Operation Desert Shield/Storm was challenging and rewarding at the same time. Because I was the chief of readiness for the 314th Civil Engineering Squadron at Little Rock AFB, Arkansas, I was the first to know our squadron might be tasked to go to the Middle East. We had approximately two weeks before we would be on our way to the United Arab Emirates (UAE), but we were ready to leave at a moment's notice during the last nine days of that period.

This was perhaps the most difficult time of all, wondering what was ahead of us. Would our equipment be adequate? How would our personal lives be affected by the separation? Were we ready for the challenges to come? The major lesson I had already learned was "never sacrifice readiness to the 'our squadron will never deploy' mind-set." Unfortunately, many people in our squadron and on our base had that mind-set. Consequently, training took a back seat, at times, to "more urgent" activities.

We performed our mission successfully; however, if the situation is more difficult next time, if hostilities begin earlier, or if we have less time to prepare, then the training and physical fitness of some of our troops may be inadequate. And so I advise my fellow service members: Always be prepared for your primary mission, even if that mission only occurs once in a career.

As soon as we stepped off the plane at our final location, the major challenge for myself and the four other officers in our 100-man Prime BEEF team was to keep morale up. Initially, we had limited tools and equipment, poor food, grossly overcrowded living conditions, and a sense that we were just a burden on the base. The troops were not

23

happy, and I found myself constantly explaining the "big picture" when I didn't know what it was. Nor did I know whether our situation would improve. I never realized how much the enlisted force depended on us for information and leadership. We spent a significant amount of time counseling and advising about personal problems back home or other situations. I had not expected this task, and frequently I found it difficult due to the complexity of the problem or just plain lack of experience in counseling on my part.

From an engineering standpoint, the experience was interesting. Our team was responsible for constructing a secure operating base for the USAF. We were on a UAE air force base, but we were given only minimal facilities. With USAF prepositioned assets, we built a tent city to billet the 1,100 troops at our base. We also built a chapel, a post office, recreational facilities, utilities, and industrial work areas for aircraft maintenance and other functions. I was the main site planner. I managed the activities of our 50-person night shift. Sixteen-hour days were normal for the first month or so. It was tremendously rewarding to design something one day and see the project completed a couple of days later. I found that the more creativity I gave to the foremen, the better job I would get in return.

My favorite project was the base theater. I designed a three-tiered wooden floor structure that supported a 60-foot-long temper tent complete with dimming lights and air conditioning. Once all the materials were on hand, I met with the night shift foremen. The project would normally have taken three days to complete. I told them that if they completed it by sunrise, they would get the following day off. They agreed, and set out to build it in record time. The work site was active all evening, and the troops enjoyed the challenge. Many did not stop to take a break all night. By about 0400 the next day, the job was complete. It was a shining example of what our team could accomplish with the proper motivation.

Other major projects involved constructing berms and roads for 1,000,000 gallons of jet fuel storage, a concrete truck loading ramp, a 1.3 megawatt power plant, a water storage and chlorination facility, and nearly one mile of eight-feet-high, four-feet-thick revetment walls. Most of the work was done in temperatures over 100°F.

Although we were fortunate to have access to a major city for materials, often we had to improvise or use alternative techniques. Some people are better at improvising than others, and many times the officers had to prompt the craftsmen to use their ingenuity. In one case, we were unable to repair a waterline rupture because the pipe we had didn't have the proper ends for joining to another pipe. We asked the local military for help. Two men in native dress arrived with a hacksaw. We gave them a piece of four-inch PVC pipe we had but could not use. They gathered waste cardboard for a small fire. Then they heated the pipe ends in the fire and forced them onto the end of the broken pipeline while the ends were still soft from the heat. Their technology was basic, but it worked when we couldn't fix it with all the technology at our disposal.

At home, the stress on developing ingenuity had been low. Consequently, many jobs were not done in the desert until the correct parts or tools were on hand. I feel that a creative-thinking work force is invaluable in that situation. We must stress the importance of creativity in peacetime to increase quality and efficiency in wartime.

These were some of the lessons I learned while involved in Desert Shield/Storm. Hopefully, we will not be tested again; but if we are, most likely it will be more difficult than this test was. Adequate training, conditioning, and preparation at home will be crucial for success.

Tracking Personnel in Camel-Lot

by

Capt Jacqueline C. Grant

On 26 September 1990, a personnel support for contingency operations (PERSCO) team boarded a tanker at Wurtsmith AFB, Michigan, and set off for Cairo West, Egypt. The five-man team had been on standby for a week when, one day before departure date, a new tasking came down. This new tasking added a sixth member—an officer! Within 24 hours, I qualified on the .38, received modified chemical warfare training, called home, "outprocessed" through my own mobility processing unit (MPU) line, and picked up a workbook that would teach me all about PERSCO. The team left in a daze.

En route to Cairo, we spent a day and a night at Moron AB, Spain. There, we retired to the club to discuss PERSCO and each member's role. We were to be joined by a PERSCO team from Grand Forks AFB, North Dakota, and I would be chief of this combined team. On a sunny Saturday, 29 September 1990, our tanker touched down. When it's belly opened, we saw nothing but sand and a few bunkers in the side of a hill. We had arrived at what would be "home" for the next seven months.

Cairo West was a refueling base that was supported by tankers from Grand Forks AFB and support personnel from an assortment of bases. After we arrived, my group took charge of the welcome team that had been assembled by the first 50 people who had arrived the day before. Our first objective was to organize the team, find our combat personnel control system (CPCS), and begin accounting for all the personnel on base. There were no buildings and no electricity. Until the tent city was built, we were housed in a hotel about 30 minutes away from the base. We took the CPCS to the hotel and had two members stay in the room with it at all times. My team did not

27

initially have a vehicle, so we had to develop a plan to count the new arrivals at Cairo West, update the CPCS back at the hotel, get our strength report to CENTAF/FWD from the American embassy (we had to use the embassy, even though it was 40–60 minutes from the base, because we had no communications support at the base), and give our wing commander an updated alpha roster. All this involved several hours of negotiating through Cairo traffic in whatever vehicle we could find.

The first few days were hectic. Sometimes, the only warning we had of new arrivals was a plane circling overhead. At night, when everyone went back to the hotel, I posted two PERSCO members at the bare base to greet any planes that might "drop in" during the night. The biggest nightmare was when people arrived at Cairo East, which was the civilian airport that required passports. People sometimes sat in that airport for 24 hours before we received embassy assistance.

The day before Halloween, we all moved out to the base and settled into our tents. We set up our office, tried out our phone lines, and were allocated a car for PERSCO (a Peugeot with lights that danced across the front). We named our new home "Camel-lot," our dining facility "Dusty's," and our club (drinking was allowed in Egypt) the "Sand Rock Cafe." Our mascot was a scorpion. By the end of November, we had settled into a routine. Our services and MWR people had gone to Germany and purchased everything we needed to keep 800-plus people happy in the desert: TVs, VCRs, and movies for our movie tent; music for the cafe; and fitness equipment for the gym. They set up Nile cruises and tours to the Sphinx, the Great Pyramids, the Cairo Museum, and Coptic Cairo. They did an outstanding job of finding things for us to do as we continued to wait. Keeping people busy as the weeks grew into months was the main focus.

Within my team, I had two areas of concern. First, I had too large a team for the population we were supporting. All the airmen were from one base and all the NCOs were from my (different) base. Initially, the airmen had difficulty taking direction from NCOs they did not know. I split the team into two shifts, a day shift and a night shift, which kept everyone busy. The day shift handled customer

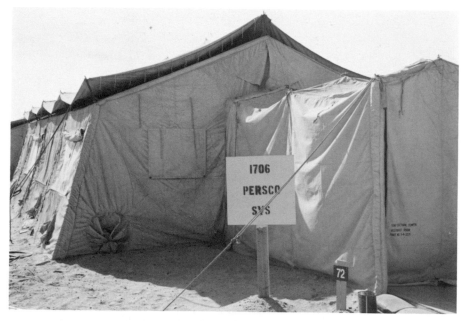

1706 PERSCO SVS

Dusty's Diner

Selling Sodas at the Sand Rock Cafe

Sand Volleyball

inquiries while the night shift handled paperwork and computer updates. Second, I established a "forum" where both shifts aired their differences and came up with their own solutions. I also called upon my three master sergeants to lead and discipline. This worked well, and the master sergeants were a great help to me. By mid-December, half the team was redeployed to Riyadh, Saudi Arabia, while my Wurtsmith team and I remained at Cairo West.

In December, we were told that the Grand Forks operations and maintenance personnel who had arrived with us would be redeployed to King Khalid and would be replaced by Guard personnel. Many of us had become close friends, and our mood was sombre. Most of us had already been there for three months, and we were becoming restless for something to happen. The only news we had was from CNN, which was not aware that we were in Egypt. To help morale, we had a New Year's Eve party. We welcomed in the new year, and then settled down to wait again.

PERSCO Tent at Christmas

Guard personnel arrived and active duty personnel departed. There was a definite period of readjustment. Many Guard personnel worried about businesses back home. They complained about the facilities at Camel-lot, to which the "regulars" took offense, as they had just spent three or four months building it from the ground up. PERSCO had no written guidance specific to Guard personnel issues, but we helped by sending messages to the home CBPOs for their action. We also acted as a go-between for Guard questions to CENTAF/FWD. The operations personnel began practicing their flights, learning the curves and bumps on the runway, and taking off with wild dogs and Egyptians strolling across the runway.

On 15 January 1991, the entire camp was tense and ready for something to happen. We knew that a message indicating when everything would begin had arrived, but no one outside the wing commander's staff knew the actual date and time. When the war began, very little changed at Cairo West. Only mission-essential messages were authorized for transmission, and we continued to send our daily strength-change message to CENTAF/FWD. We began using letters to check on day-to-day questions, such as the status of career job reservations and promotion increment numbers. We practiced our casualty reporting procedures, ran daily alpha rosters, and ensured that our hard copy backup files were accurate. For the duration of the contingency, all base personnel were confined to the base. MWR continued to bend over backwards to entertain us, and the club became the hot spot of the camp. The security police stood guard all day and all night along the perimeter of our camp. As the nighttime temperature dropped, the first sergeant instigated a program called "soup for the troops." Officers and senior NCOs volunteered to take hot soup out to each bunker and spend time talking with the troops. It was very good for their morale because it made them feel appreciated. For our part, we had no idea how cold and lonely the perimeter was. We no longer complained about our jobs or working conditions after that.

When we heard the war was over, the operations personnel celebrated and everyone began thinking about going home. After a few weeks, we learned that Cairo West would probably stay open as a refueling station for the redeployment effort. We immediately began processing decorations. By the time the redeployment began, we had forwarded all the decorations to CENTAF/FWD. PERSCO became deeply involved in helping commanders receive information about rotating their troops home. We sent messages identifying all the troops who had met their 179-day point, and we requested replacements. Gradually, we received messages indicating that replacements would be sent for the personnel identified . . . all but my PERSCO team. HQ SAC told us there were no teams available to replace us since almost every base in SAC had deployed at least one PERSCO team. Morale was low for my team as spouses began calling and writing to find out when we were coming home. When we found out that the 379th Wing (our home wing) had redeployed home and that the town and the base had hosted a huge homecoming party, it was even harder. Luckily, though, we were so busy trying to painlessly "outprocess" the "old" personnel and "inprocess" their replacements that we had little time to mope.

We developed a good out-processing system. We forwarded projected departure lists to various base agencies instead of asking each person to outprocess through each agency. We built packages for each member, explaining how our location affected their benefits, including imminent danger pay, unit-essential messing, and verification of length of stay in the AOR. Once the members turned in their Egyptian identification cards, they received their package. The transportation personnel gave us copies of their manifests to compare with our departure lists. Our arrival/departure messages were extensive, but we maintained an accurate count at all times.

At the last minute, we received word that my team would be replaced. I began sending my folks home until there were only two of us left from the original group. The new team came from various bases, and we began orienting them as soon as they arrived. We had acquired an amazing number of responsibilities during our seven months: processing Egyptian identification cards, maintaining the alcoholic beverage ration cards, assisting MWR personnel with tours, and helping services personnel to staff their on-base gift shop. We passed on our procedures and shortcuts, and introduced the team to the Egyptians with whom we had been working. To get Egyptian ID cards, US military ID cards were taken to the Egyptian camp and used to fill out a blank card (English on one side, Arabic on the other side). Photo copies were made of both, and the Egyptian security commander signed them. This wasn't a bad procedure for one or two, but frequently we had 50 to 100 people arrive simultaneously.

Without a good system, and trust between my team and theirs, it would have been chaos. The Egyptians constantly ran out of cards, could not find the person who needed to sign them, or had a copy machine that would not work. As they got to know us, they began trusting us to take the cards with us, make copies on our machines, and return the copies to them. They kept strict track of each card and, prior to each plane's departure, reviewed a copy of the manifest and questioned every card that was not returned to them. Several people tried to leave with their cards (for souvenirs), which caused problems for us with Egyptian security. Much of what we accomplished came from the working relationships we had developed with the Egyptians.

Operation Desert Shield/Storm taught me about my own patriotism, leadership, initiative, and creativity in problem solving. It gave me a crash course on how to work with and respect enlisted personnel that OTS could only hint at. It showed me that I could get guidance from my superiors, and that I was not expected to know everything simply because I was "team chief." Several captains and majors helped with basic things they knew from experience. It was difficult to adjust to "going by the book" again at home. Even though it was a long seven months, I'm glad I participated.

An Air Force Flies on Its Stomach

by

Capt Rhonda D. Perry

With much fanfare, we were delivered to the C-130 that would take us to Dover Air Force Base (AFB), Delaware. Before I boarded, a reporter asked me if I had any last words. "No," I said, and kept moving.

I recorded that significant moment on 30 August 1990, shortly after the wheels of our C-130 cleared the pavement of Charleston International Airport.

I got to ride up front with the crew so I had the best seat. Not so my folks. I had become troop commander for 48 pax-services, transportation, and somebody else I can't remember.

At the time, none of us knew that the wheels of an airplane carrying us home wouldn't touch down for the next 213 days. For the members of the 437th Services Squadron's Prime RIBS (Readiness in Base Services) team, deployment to the Persian Gulf had just begun.

My first impressions of Seeb, Oman (who had ever heard of Oman, anyway?), were formed as I jumped from the side exit of a C-130 in the early morning hours of 3 September 1990. Not even a light breeze stirred, and at 0530 it was already hot. Scanning my surroundings, I saw nothing but brown mountains in the distance, obscured by a brown sandy haze and brown scrawny "trees" on the horizon. Most of all, nothing moved except us on that giant slab of cement somewhere in the middle of nowhere. As members of my squadron joined me on the tarmac, I could see many of them clutching their orders almost like a shield. Our orders read "length of deployment 90 days," but I knew in my heart we'd be there much longer.

Members of the March AFB Prime BEEF and RIBS team had set up camp about 10 days before support personnel, maintenance, and aircrews arrived. By the time we arrived, it looked just like "the book" said it should. Temper tents were staked in neat rows, and we could clearly see the form of an operational base. The first day of our arrival was a momentous occasion for the 400-plus members of "Camp Nacirema" (American spelled backwards). They'd been eating MREs because they were without power in the 9-1 Harvest Eagle kitchen tent. A KC-135 aircrew made a quick trip to the United Arab Emirates (UAE), and that night a full shift of cooks prepared "gourmet" hamburgers for a very hungry camp. They said it was the best meal they'd ever eaten.

The first week of our desert experience was spent organizing and adjusting to Camp Nacirema. We left Charleston as the 437th Services Squadron, but now found ourselves in an encampment composed of several hundred people from all over the Air Force. We had no choice but to lay aside squadron and command loyalties, curb egos and personal pride, and merge our expertise and talents into the 1702d Aerial Refueling Wing (Provisional).

1702d AREFW(P) Services Squadron

I began my tour as the "deputy chief of services," but I became "the boss" after our major returned home on emergency leave. Our task was to turn our desert encampment into a bustling, thriving wing capable of supporting 1,500-plus people. Everything I'd ever learned about "being in the field" came in handy, and believe me, we had our work cut out for us!

Our first priority (by way of unanimous vote from the camp) was to create quality, tasty meals in a less than desirable environment. A contract had been established with the Royal Air Force of Oman catering unit to provide fresh vegetables, fruits, meats, breads, and various other items. We were thankful for their help; otherwise, we would have eaten a steady diet of B-rations broken only by the obligatory MRE.

The creative juices of our most talented chefs kicked into high gear. It's amazing how skilled a cook becomes at preparing "mundane" items like pork chops, hamburger, and chicken day after day. Even more astonishing was their ability to prepare steak, pizza, lobster (yes, I said lobster—they were delicious), and deli sandwiches in a field environment. But we didn't stop there—our chefs put on their thinking caps and created some of the best brownies, cobbler, cake, and cookies you've ever wrapped your teeth around! We staged cookouts for a camp population of over 1,500, and we sponsored monthly "ice-cream socials." If you think that sounds good, the Thanksgiving and Christmas meals were feasts. The cooks worked two days to prepare ham, turkey, roast beef, mashed potatoes and gravy, yams, assorted vegetables, and some delicious pies that rivaled grandma's. If I sound proud of the accomplishments of "my" troops—I am!

Our camp did more than just eat—services soon became expert at providing "luxuries." Camp residents wanted clean clothes, and "Suds-R-Us" was born. We opened business with two sets of field washers and dryers, and eventually worked our way up to four sets as the camp population grew. At the height of production, we were cleaning 500 bags of laundry a day! Now, anybody who has worked long around field equipment knows how cantankerous it can be—the dryer units decided it was too hot, gritty, and just plain hard work to function in the desert sun, so they quit. From that time on, the camp dried its clothes as our forefathers did—with solar heat.

Perhaps the greatest challenge we faced was establishing and maintaining a well-stocked "Tactical Field Exchange" (TFE) and troop issue warehouse. Prime FARE (commissary personnel) from Illinois operated these functions flawlessly. We ordered goods from AAFES in Dhahran, and when they could no longer keep us supplied, we bought goods on the Oman economy for resale in the TFE. By the end of our seven-and-one-half-month tour, Camp Nacirema residents had purchased thousands of dollars in goods—the highest in the theater.

We've all heard the phrase "flexibility is the key to air power." During the middle of December 1990, we flexed. I was finishing dinner when we learned that 400 Army medical personnel (unscheduled for Camp Nacirema) would take up residence on our small patch of desert in less than 48 hours. This wouldn't have been so bad except that almost 500 hospital personnel from Scott AFB were scheduled to arrive in two weeks. "Where are we going to put all these people?" was my first thought. When the Army arrived, we temporarily billeted them in the Air Force hospital tents while CE turned a warehouse into a huge dormitory. We expanded the dining, serving, and storage areas of the "LeMay Inn," and all other services, to meet our new guests' needs. At that point, the 1702d AREFW Services Division totalled 75 personnel from seven different bases and two separate branches of service.

Of course, no field deployment would be complete without visits from commanding officers and high-ranking officials. The guests who visited Camp Nacirema (and ate at the LeMay Inn) included Gen H. Norman Schwarzkopf; chief of staff of the Air Force, Gen Merrill A. McPeak; Central Air Force Commander Lt Gen Charles Horner; and Chief Master Sergeant of the Air Force Pfingston.

As Camp Nacirema grew in size, we waited expectantly for 15 January. Most of us had been deployed since August and, quite frankly, we were ready to get the show on the road! I'll never forget the moment the war began for members of the 1702d. A group of us were playing cards on the "porch" of one of the tents. We looked up to see several crew members walking down "Main Street" in their sanitized flight suits, concentrated expressions on their faces. Though the camp wasn't briefed about their activity, we knew the time had come. I thought to myself, "These are my friends, and they're ready to fly off to war." Those first hours of war were long ones for all of us—we were concerned about the welfare of "our" aircrews, concerned about how Saddam would react. I think the entire camp crowded into the TV room to watch as CNN reported on the war as it happened.

Over the next 42 days, our tiny, quiet patch of desert became a springboard for refueling the many different aircraft participating in the war. Camp services shifted into high gear to meet the needs of the mission. We instituted 24-hour hot meal service for mission-essential personnel and pilots. "Suds-R-Us" and the TFE expanded hours of operation for those working 12-hour-plus shifts.

The challenges we faced in turning a bare base into a livable situation are too numerous to detail, but it's impossible to paint an accurate picture of our part in the Gulf War without telling something about the "off-duty" story as well. Halfway through my tour, we came up with a theory about how "newbies" (new personnel) adjusted to life in Camp Nacirema when they arrived. There seemed to be five stages that people went through. The first stage was DENIAL. Persons in the DENIAL stage flatly refused to acknowledge they had actually deployed to Oman, lived in a tent, slept on a cot, showered with hundreds of people, ate MREs for lunch, and had to keep their mouths closed for fear of sand. The second phase was the OK-I'M-HERE-BUT- I'M-NOT-SUPPOSED -TO-BE-AND-MY-SQUADRON-WILL-RESCUE-ME-ANY-TIME-NOW stage. With the third stage came a dose of reality: the OK-I'M-HERE-SO-I-MAY-AS-WELL-NOT-BE-MISERABLE-BUT-I'M-NOT-GOING-TO-OVERDO-IT stage. People begin to take on life again—some actually began to laugh! The forth stage held the greatest reward because people decided to become active again. That was the I'M-HERE-NOW-SO-I-MAY-AS-WELL-CON-TRIBUTE stage. The fifth phase was the best: I'M-SHORT-AND-NOTHING-CAN-TOUCH-ME-NOW-AMERICA-HERE-I-COME.

We became adept at all kinds of games: cards, volleyball, trivial pursuit, horseshoes, pool, monopoly (my personal favorite), Scrabble, foosball, Ping-Pong, and darts—everybody's most-practiced game. We read books (I read at least 20), watched CNN, movies, exercised, socialized, and even resorted to putting together puzzles on New Year's Eve.

Drawing down the camp was an experience that elated our minds and hearts. My Combat Support Group (CSG) commander came to me on the morning of 5 April and told me that if we could take the dining facility down and pack it within a day, we could be on the KC-10 flight that was leaving the following day. It was amazing how quickly tents and temporary buildings came down when the carrot of the United States was dangled before us. We'd already decided how to cut back on hot meal service, so we were prepared for anything. I told my troops the news at 0700; by 1400 that afternoon, there was absolutely no indication that the LeMay Inn had ever existed.

Through our experiences, we gained so much more than we knew at the time. We learned about ourselves professionally because, when the "chips were down," we accomplished tremendous things in a short period of time. We learned about each other, and in order to "survive" we had to share everything from toothpaste (when somebody's resupply care package didn't arrive) to space in an "office" 10 times too small for one person. We shared feelings of loneliness, homesickness, happiness, and anticipation, and we made life bearable for each other. We learned so much about ourselves—about strengths, weaknesses, good things, and things we'd rather not have known. Finally, we learned about time. Though our time in Oman passed too slowly, we knew this old saying held true about Desert Storm: "This too shall pass."

In the year since our return from the Persian Gulf, my memory of Camp Nacirema has faded. I can't see faces as clearly, or remember names I swore I'd never forget. I can't "taste" the food or "feel" the heat of the desert anymore. What I still remember vividly, though, is the sound of people's laughter, special quotes, or gestures. And I'll never, ever, forget the (sometimes tough) lessons I learned about being an officer and a leader during that historical moment in our nation's history. To the men and women who served with the 1702d Aerial Refueling Wing at Seeb Air Base, Oman, you'll know what I mean when I say it's good to be home in America, "where the dart board has no wind."

Creating an Attitude:
A Security Police Perspective

by

Capt Jim Marry

I arrived in Saudi Arabia on 7 August 1990. I stayed there for over seven months, working as a Security Police flight commander. I led from 43 troops at the start of the deployment to more than 100 by the end of the war. Our mission was to secure base resources and personnel against hostile ground threats. Unfortunately, our peacetime training did not apply to wartime requirements—a situation that created some difficulty and stress.

I had learned during a police tactical team seminar conducted by the FBI that people react to extreme stress in one of three ways: they do what they were trained to do, they panic, or they do whatever they last had on their mind. During Desert Shield/Storm, I learned that security policemen tend to do the last thing they had on their mind.

During peacetime, we trained the way our doctrine and dogma said we would fight. We planned to draw a line around the base and stop intruders at the line. We divided the base into sectors and assigned a 44-member air base ground defense flight to each sector. Our 206-series regulations told us how each flight would defend its sector: organized into a clear structure of squads and fire teams. Fighting positions were dug on the perimeter to give depth to the defense, coordination points were established to provide boundaries between adjacent flights, and fields of fire were interlocked. Communication was essential. Cohesion was essential, too, and these security police flights came from every base and command of the Air Force. Regulations directed that they be placed under a single defense force commander who would tie it all together.

We followed this religiously—sort of. We had done something completely different during day-to-day peacetime activities. We weren't even organized the same. But when we trained for war, this was it. All the formal schools taught it. Our unit training section had a designated NCO to teach it. Programs such as Silver Flag-Alpha and Volant Scorpion were run to train entire units to do it. Despite the regulations, the schools, and the programs, however, I had trained for war only once with the flight I took to Saudi—we defended a one-kilometer-long sector in the woods, a few miles from base.

The mission we performed was very different from what we had prepared to do. In prewar practice, we defended territory and equipment. In the desert, the majority of our effort was directed towards protecting people. The terrain, the mission, the equipment, and the available troops necessitated a fluid, mobile, responsive defense—the antithesis of our prewar training and doctrine.

My assigned sector in the war covered 48 square kilometers. The ground was either sheet rock or sugar sand—both impossible to dig foxholes into. For the first month, we had three vehicles: an HMMWV, a Chevy Blazer we borrowed from a civilian, and a flatbed truck (I never asked how we got that). Our radios could communicate over one or two kilometers, not twelve or fifteen. Coordinating with the one adjacent SP flight was impossible—they weren't anywhere near us. Integrating with the adjacent Army MPs, Army Patriot Batteries, Marine Corps ADAG, Royal Saudi Air Police, Royal Saudi Army, and Royal Air Force Regiment (UK) required finesse, imagination, and bartering.

Since we were unable to do what we were trained to do, we did what we had on our minds last: we acted like we were at our home base, where we used the squad concept only when we lived in foxholes. In Saudi Arabia, since we weren't living in foxholes as we had trained, the flight's squad and fire team organization was immediately thrown out.

Halfway through Desert Shield, a replacement operations officer came in. He de-sectored the base and demanded eight-hour shifts, completely destroying what remained of the wartime organizational structure. And even after the units were combined, one lieutenant would still talk only to troops from his home base. Another captain was willing to talk to all the troops—endlessly complaining about

Cooperative Security

how the deployment was interfering with her plans to attend law school.

We were mentally stuck on our home base in terms of the mission, too. We had to protect people—something new, which required innovation and resourcefulness. We ended up protecting people as if they were airplanes.

I had to lead my troops away from this mess and ensure that nobody "choked" if things went bad. I had to bring them into the present. They needed confidence in their abilities. They had to know exactly what they could or could not expect. They needed a war-fighting attitude.

To establish this attitude, the flight sergeant and I gave the troops something new to think about. First, we set priorities of work and daily routines. Every day, there was something immediate that needed to be accomplished collectively—build shelters, fill sandbags, run communication lines, clean and check equipment, etc. This plan gave the troops something to do besides stand on post and think about being miserable.

Next, we emphasized the reality of what was happening. We played the "what if" game continuously. What if there is an attack? What if there is a terrorist in the next vehicle? What if someone comes over this fence? This game forced the troops to think about where they were and what they were doing. It forced them to have presence of mind, to be aware of the here and now. Every day, the flight sergeant closed guardmount with, "Remember—keep the edge!"

Finally, to set the attitude, I delegated to the lowest level. In peacetime, junior NCOs don't get many opportunities to take responsibility. By delegating down, I drove home the point that everyone had a stake in what went on. Even the most junior NCO was expected to make decisions. To do this, I forced my sector to reorganize back into a squad structure similar to what we had used in training. Consequently, everyone knew exactly where they fit.

Protecting Our Aircraft

When the troops started showing the "right attitude," we started training. If things got bad, they would need something to keep them from reverting back to whatever they were thinking last. I didn't reinvent any wheels to do this. I just drew on what they had already been taught. For instance, they knew that a highly visible patrol car with a radar gun deters speeding. Extending this concept, we used highly visible HMMWVs with machine guns to deter violence. I emphasized that they knew everything they needed to know, it was just going to be applied differently.

Once we established what we wanted to do and how we intended to do it, we rehearsed. In peacetime we exercise—it implies practice for something remote and extraordinary. Exercising is a sort of evaluation. We ask, "Can we do something?" Rehearsal implies something definite, specific, and immediate. In prewar training, we learned how to patrol. Before going on a patrol, we rehearsed actions toward the objective. At least for the SP, rehearsal means "we will do exactly this." So, my flight rehearsed our defense daily, perfecting our response to every "if" we could think of.

The lesson from all this is clear: Train like you plan to fight. Because we seldom trained for our wartime mission, and what we practiced was somewhat naive, we had no choice but to fall back on what we knew best—peacetime operations, the last thing that had been on our minds.

For me, most of the war is as distant as the wars I read about in history books. When I think of the war, I don't conjure images of the big picture, massive air strikes, spectacular bomb runs, or tanks charging across the desert. As a company grade officer in charge of part of the security on one base, a small cog in a huge machine, I didn't need to worry about all that. I worried about 40 guys and where they fit into that 100 kilometers of space and few months of time. I worried about an attitude.

Red Horse in the Desert

by

Capt Jeth A. Fogg

My experience with Operation Desert Shield/Storm started on 26 October 1990. I flew commercial air to Philadelphia, Pennsylvania, then took a taxi to Dover AFB, Delaware. At Dover we arranged for military airlift of 34 personnel to the theater of operations for the following day. Once the 34 personnel arrived at Dover, we palletized our gear and loaded on the C-5 Galaxy for the long flight to the theater of operations.

I spent the first couple of days in Riyadh, Saudi Arabia, then traveled to Shaikh Isa Air Base (AB), Bahrain, to study the feasibility of erecting metal bin revetments in order to harden the parking areas for F-4G Wild Weasels. After one week in-country, we started erecting metal bin revetments on the south taxiway loop of Shaikh Isa AB. RED HORSE provided the necessary knowledge and skill; Prime BEEF and aircraft maintenance personnel provided labor. After three weeks of construction, RED HORSE was tasked with a much larger project.

I was at King Fahd AB, Saudi Arabia, when I was notified of the new construction project. En route to Shaikh Isa, I heard the details and several proposals of the provisional wing commander, Colonel Karp. United States RF-4C aircraft were going to be deployed to the location. RED HORSE would construct a parking ramp, adjoining taxiway, and the area necessary for mission support facilities for this specialized aircraft. When I arrived, I discussed the plans with the base civil engineer, Lieutenant Colonel Shoemaker.

The plan was broken down into three phases. Phase I had to be completed by the first of January, before the first aircraft were deployed. It was a 550-foot by 204-foot concrete hardstand with a

100-foot-wide connecting asphalt taxiway that circled the hardstand and tied into the airfield's main taxiway. Once completed, phase I would provide revetted parking for 20 F-4s. Phase II was a 450-foot by 240-foot concrete hardstand with adjoining taxiway. This would provide 16 additional revetted parking slots. The phase II taxiway would be tied into the existing south loop taxiway, providing two exits from the hardstand area in case one exit was obstructed by unexploded ordnance (UXO), craters, or unmovable aircraft.

RED HORSE had eight personnel on the project when construction started, and their first priority was earthwork. Immediately, we knew that we needed some very heavy equipment. The time line and the severe soil conditions required equipment that was much larger than anything in the USAF inventory. Calling on the expertise of MSgt Paul Desarkisian, we came up with an estimate of the equipment we needed to do the job. Construction would start as soon as we had the earth-moving equipment, and we soon had the equipment because we had an excellent relationship with a civilian contractor who had the equipment nearby. Due to line-haul restraints, the long distance from Riyadh, and slow border-crossing procedures, mobilizing RED HORSE equipment took a little longer.

Once the rented Caterpillar D-9 bulldozers were on site, we pushed off loose topsoil to give us a better idea of what we were up against. We found several limestone ridges and immediately started cutting them down, using three rented Caterpillar 225 excavators with hammer attachments. In Bahrain, this piece of equipment is fondly called a "rockbreaker." Once the limestone ridges were fractured, we used the large D-9 bulldozers with single tooth ripper attachments to tear out the fractured rock and push it off to the side.

We first raised and leveled (brought to grade) the site for the concrete hardstand so we could set the concrete forms and place the concrete. We learned some hard lessons on our first concrete pour. In the US, we used concrete trucks that had three or more chute extensions, enabling us to place the concrete within the forms in a timely manner. In Bahrain, the trucks had only two chutes, so the pour was far slower and much more laborious than we anticipated. A supervisor from the concrete company suggested a concrete pumper truck to

Caterpillar 225 "Rockbreakers"

place the concrete. This solved our problems. Two concrete trucks unloaded into the pumper truck simultaneously, and the pumper placed the concrete between the form work. At the same time, we were preparing the area for asphalt paving.

After the concrete work was completed, the paving operation began. We had two Cedar Rapids pavers, 20 asphalt delivery trucks, and several rollers. The paving operation went smoothly except for one glitch. Following the daytime operations, the host base spent the night erecting metal bin revetments on the completed concrete hardstand. This procedure was great for completing both tasks simultaneously, but the fuel leaking from the "lightalls" broke down the fresh asphalt. Therefore, we moved all the lightalls off the asphalt and patched the damaged areas. On the final day of construction for phase I, we were placing asphalt on the photo reconnaissance support area, patching eroded lightall spots, and watching the RF-4C aircraft taxi into their new home of concrete, asphalt, and steel.

51

Concrete Pumper Truck Operating into the Evening

Asphalt Operations in Bahrain

The phase II area was almost at grade and ready for concrete forms when rain turned the area to mud. Construction was halted for one week while we waited for the area to dry out. Since we felt the air war might begin soon, RED HORSE personnel helped build Prime BEEF-designed bunkers and earthen berms on base. In the meantime, our RED HORSE equipment was recalled to Riyadh to form combat repair teams in the event base recovery throughout the theater became necessary. We substituted rental equipment and pressed on with construction when the soil dried out.

When the earth-moving crew completed the earthwork for the second hardstand area, the daytime asphalt/concrete crew started. Concrete forms and concrete were alternately placed on a 24-hour schedule. The nighttime crew concentrated on earthwork and concrete work. Working around the clock, we met the strict phase I deadlines. We learned the "lightall on asphalt" lesson from phase I, and we noticed that the F-4s lost some fuel from their wing tips when they pressurized their fuel tanks—JP-4 fuel on relatively fresh asphalt lessens its durability. To solve this problem, we increased the depth of each

Nighttime Concrete Placement

concrete-revetted parking spot by 20 feet. This provided a location for lightalls and an area for pressurizing fuel tanks.

Early in the morning of 17 January 1991, I kept awakening to the sound of jets taking off from the airfield. The quantity of aircraft was far greater than the normal air traffic for this time of day and I knew that the air war had begun. I realized the true consequence of the air war a couple of hours later when we had our first Scud alert. We had another Scud alert later in the morning, and we averaged three or four per day through 22 January 1991. In those first few days of the air war, we heard one Scud hit Dhahran, about 30 miles across the water. After 22 January, the alerts weren't as frequent. This helped put our sleep schedule back in order. At this point, I felt that the air war was going well, a feeling soon confirmed by CNN and the local intelligence briefings.

The Navy Seabees stationed with us at Shaikh Isa AB were forward-deployed, so we figured something was up and we might be the next group to hit the road north. I discussed this topic with my senior NCOs, and we decided that we had better be ready to go if we were tasked to recover forward airfields in Iraq. We planned convoy packages, weapons, and fuel to get us there. The tasking to move north and recover never came, but we were ready.

Once the Navy Seabees left, food quality on base diminished. We brought in five RED HORSE cooks and a mobile kitchen trailer (MKT) from Riyadh. That enhanced food quality and sped the construction process by reducing travel time to eat. We also set up our own laundry unit, using two washers and dryers like you might have in your own home. Power was supplied by a lightall, water by a water buffalo that was pressurized by a pump from a fuel blivet set. This unit was more efficient than the base's contract laundry system. Now we had clean clothes and didn't have to worry about losing them.

All our mechanics were instrumental in keeping our equipment up and running, and the contractor's mechanics helped repair USAF assets on several occasions. Although these mechanics were on base full-time, we had no gas masks for them. This typically wasn't a problem because most Scud alerts occurred during the night, but in one instance we had a midday Scud alert. Everyone ran into the

Field Laundry Unit

bunker, contractor's mechanics included, and the military members put on their gas masks. The contractor's mechanics stood there mask-less. This raised a true moral dilemma that the base disaster preparedness people couldn't handle. We ordered two masks from Riyadh and signed them out daily to the contractor mechanics.

The disaster preparedness people had an effective Scud alert system. The only time we knew it didn't work was on 22 February 1991 when we were awakened by a Patriot missile intercepting a Scud within three miles of the air base. They must have fixed the system, because we heard the alarm again on 25 February—and we heard the Scud impact the Army barracks in Dhahran.

After completing phase II, we changed personnel. Ten of our personnel were on the RED HORSE explosive demolition team that went north to explosively deny two Iraqi airfields. This posed a slight problem for the project because the demolition team contained two key senior NCOs. However, the experience and leadership of the junior NCOs shined brightly. Phase III earthwork was already under way when we encountered a stubborn limestone ridge at the intersection of phases II and III. But the contractor had over 200 excavators with hammers on the base to cut out the limestone rock. After removing the ridge, we placed the base coarse, brought it to final grade, and paved the remainder of the taxiway in two sections, one-half each time. Finally, we painted the stripes and the project was complete.

We spent one and one-half days loading equipment and putting things back together. The cooks had already flown back, and our small encampment was closing down. We convoyed the remaining equipment back to Riyadh, leaving early Tuesday morning, 11 March 1991. After a slow 10 hours that included several mechanical breakdowns, we arrived in Riyadh. On Wednesday I wrote a short project summary, packed my gear, and boarded a bus to King Fahd. On Thursday morning, I climbed aboard a C-5 Galaxy and flew home. It was absolutely fantastic to be home with my wife-to-be.

The $4.4 million project at Shaikh Isa AB was the largest in RED HORSE history. It established several RED HORSE construction

"Courtesy RED HORSE"

records, including most concrete placed in a single day (696 cubic yards) and most asphalt placed in a single day (2,200 tons).

I learned three valuable lessons from this project:

(1) USAF equipment is too small for completing heavy earth-moving construction projects in a timely manner. The Air Force should have construction equipment that is highly mobile and air-liftable for small, short-duration construction deployments, and it should have large, sealift-size equipment for large, long-duration construction projects.

(2) Heavy construction equipment should be purchased from well-established companies that have worldwide parts distribution systems. The contractor's Caterpillar equipment was never down for parts. We had a brand new USAF dump truck that operated one day before its hydraulic pump burned up. The pump should have been an off-the-shelf item, but it took two months to repair the truck because we couldn't get the part.

(3) The line-haul capability of RED HORSE should be enhanced. During the Gulf War, the squadron was centrally located in Riyadh and had to convoy its equipment assets throughout the theater. This arrangement spread line-haul assets thin, slowing construction. A greater line-haul capability would vastly enhance our mobility and our ability to move as a unit.

The Shaikh Isa parking ramp and taxiway project imposed difficult time lines and tough environmental conditions on both man and machine. The one thing that made this project happen was the "Can Do, Will Do," hard-working attitude of RED HORSE personnel.

Transportation and Maintenance at King Fahd

by

Capt Rob A. Scofidio

After arriving at King Fahd International Airport, I made my way out to the flight line to find our aircraft generation squadron (AGS) commander, Lieutenant Colonel Loyd. She was about the busiest person out on the flight line, and lots of work needed to be done. Colonel Loyd told Lt Steve Williams and me to work with the acting transportation squadron commander, Second Lieutenant Johnson, who was transporting support equipment and supplies to the flight line, supply area, and tent city.

Many transport aircraft were unloading their contents of people and cargo at King Fahd, but the transportation personnel did not know where the different types of cargo belonged on the flight line. Our main job was to get equipment such as all terrain (AT) forklifts and flatbed trucks to the transportation folks. We did this in conjunction with the mobile aerial port squadron (MAPS), which was responsible for unloading the transport aircraft as they arrived. The guys at the MAPS supported us in any way they could. They loaded our flatbed trucks when they could, and they furnished us with AT drivers at other times. Unfortunately, the ATs broke down, and we didn't have the parts to fix them. It was difficult to unload and load aircraft with just a couple of those monster forklifts in working order. Nevertheless, the ATs moved their massive pallets so quickly between flatbed trucks that I imagined myself being run over or speared.

Fortunately, we had a truck to get around in. We put more than 3,000 miles on the truck in just under three weeks of work. I worked the noon-to-midnight shift, and Steve worked opposite me. We sat down with Lieutenant Johnson and discussed a plan of attack for our upcoming job. Transportation operated from a maintenance operations center (MOC), or dispatch, which directed drivers to different locations. I could talk with them over a fair distance when the atmospheric conditions were right for our radios. We planned to dispatch drivers with their flatbeds to the MAPS area to await aircraft. MAPS would load the flatbeds with similar pallets so that one truck could unload at one area rather than traveling to several. After the truck was unloaded, the driver returned to the MAPS area to repeat the process. Variables included the availability of ATs at the unloading locations. We planned to place forklifts at various locations to download the trucks when they arrived, but we lacked the forklifts to do this.

Steve and I worked with the transportation squadron for almost three weeks. I spent the majority of my time between vehicle maintenance, MAPS, and the flight line. We all had radios by this time, so I could communicate with both dispatch and the road chief. At noon the heat was nearly unbearable, so my shift began in some shady or cool place waiting for Steve to show up with the truck. After driving to the MOC area, Steve would explain the events of the previous night and morning. We would discuss the present situation and equipment availability. The transportation personnel were in the middle of shift change as well, so we wouldn't see much going on at this time. Usually, the MOC area was beginning to fill up with equipment pallets, and transportation aircraft were either waiting to take off or waiting to unload their precious cargo. Steve and I would inventory the different pallets, and I would form some sort of game plan for separating the pallets into groups for loading and transporting to their respective areas. The equipment—tents, assorted generators, and other tent-city-related materiel—that came in on the C-130s was unbelievable. After I got a good rundown from Steve, I'd take him back to the hooch for his 12-hour rest. Since he had no air-conditioning, I wondered when he slept. Then I'd run around trying to coordinate my game plan.

We lost the most time during the transportation shift changes. By the time the new drivers, dispatchers, and road chiefs got going, we were usually at least two hours into our shift. I always picked up a few radio batteries from the flight line MOC to ensure that I could make it through the evening hours. Later, the transportation folks gave me one of their radios so I could contact their dispatch directly. Since I had to know where the road chief was because he "had a handle on" all the drivers and vehicles, radios were crucial.

Another responsibility was to bring "pax" buses and flatbeds to the MOC side so they could carry passengers and their gear to billeting. The problem was how to get a good arrival time on incoming aircraft. The MAPS people were good at giving us arrival times, but the jets very rarely came in at those times. When we knew for sure when the next transport was due, we'd get the buses and trucks there as soon as possible. Most transport aircraft were dedicated for cargo and a few passengers. I would usually load up the troop commander, and as many others as I could fit in the back of my truck, and haul them to the billeting tent.

Tent City (TC) didn't have any paved driving surfaces at this time, so vehicles traveling through stirred up immense clouds of dust that dirtied everything. People walking back from the lone shower tent had to cross several roads, and often they returned to their tents just as dirty as when they left. The posted five mph speed limit throughout TC didn't seem to help. Everything in every tent had a thick coat of dust on it. Because many tents didn't have air-conditioning, the tent doors were kept open and the dust flew in. Nobody won the war against the dust, however, no matter how tightly their tent was buttoned up.

The round-trip distance between the MOC side and TC was 10 miles. Miles quickly accumulated as I made between five and 10 round-trips, plus other side trips, on my shift. When a jet taxied up, I climbed up the troop ladder to the troop compartment to find out the number of troops and their base. Then I called for transportation, led them off the jet, and briefed them on what to expect while deployed. After the briefing, we loaded up my truck and other trucks with personal gear, boarded the buses, and headed off. My goal was to clear the MOC ramp of pallets before Steve came to work.

My truck also served as a tow vehicle. I transported all sorts of aircraft engines and aerospace ground equipment (AGE) to our side, and to the 23d TFW side, of the ramp. I also carried bomb trailers over to the munitions storage area (MSA). We took gasoline over to the MOC side to fill up the bomb lifts, or "jammers," for the long ride over to the maintenance side. It would take a jammer nearly an hour to make its way over to the ramp. On one occasion, a jammer overheated and we had to wait for evening before we could take it over to the other side.

As the MOC ramp filled with pallets for different organizations, I struggled to separate pallets according to their destinations. As time went on, transportation learned the different destinations, but we lost forklifts and tractor trailers to maintenance problems. Whoever was using the AT thought they owned it. At that time, we only had one operating forklift, so the pallets sat. However, MAPS did its best to support us by loading our flatbeds.

I remember eating MREs sitting in my truck cab in the hot sun. I'd place the main course out in the truck bed where the sun would heat it. Many of us placed the main courses in the truck's defrost/heating duct. It was so hot during the middle of the day that my chocolate-covered cookies always melted. I became accustomed to drinking hot water. I used Gatorade and the little Kool Aid packs that occasionally came in the MREs.

I always felt funny carrying two radios. Keeping the radios charged was difficult at first because the chargers did not work properly in the heat. After the tents were air-conditioned, batteries were easier to find. Radio performance was marginal at best, even with good batteries. Finally, my task was finished. We had received the majority of our supplies and equipment. I returned to the flight line.

It took me a little while to get to know everyone in the Falcons again after I returned from my LG experience. Working with transportation had taken my mind away from what I normally did, and these people now seemed like strangers even though we had worked many hours together before. I worked from 2300 to 1100 every day. MSgt Cal Wyatt was our night production supervisor.

The flying schedule was minimal, but since General Horner had visited our base and was upset because we had not dispersed our aircraft properly ("This is not RED FLAG!" he was rumored to have said), we worked on aircraft dispersal and personnel bunker placement.

We were also making bunkers in the ground behind the MOC. The basic parking plan had the Panthers on the eastern end of the ramp with their aircraft dispersed on the ramp in front of the terminal building. Our aircraft maintenance unit (AMU) tents were situated on the northern side of the ramp at the western end. We had moved our tent from the eastern end just adjacent to the Panthers' AMU tent to be near the MOC, then to its present spot near the alert tents.

My basic responsibilities as the assistant OIC were to motivate people to prepare fortifications, deal with people problems, and track aircraft status. Our people held up very well, even though they didn't know when they would be going home and communication between home and Saudi was sketchy at best. I was extremely impressed with how well the majority of our personnel handled the amount of work they did. We worked seven days a week, 12 hours per day, for the first six weeks we were there. Aircraft were easy to follow because we flew a limited flying schedule at first; like a "2 turn 2," for example. Gradually we worked up to a "10 turn 8" and sometimes more. Our aircraft held up well to the conditions. Since we had a priority status in parts, we kept most jets fully mission-capable. In late September, I became the OIC of the Panther AMU. Moving over to the Panthers was simple; getting to know the people and their aircraft was more difficult.

The Panthers had some good people, and I was fortunate to have the best NCOIC possible and an able assistant OIC. They knew their people and aircraft, and they were great at getting the very best out of them. In November and January, we had a few extensive exercises in preparation for the upcoming storm; the people and the aircraft performed admirably. During November and December, my NCOIC was at home on emergency leave and I got my first taste of running an AMU without immediate help. Fortunately, the Panther people knew how to do their jobs—from airman on up. Despite my chief's absence, we managed to keep our statistics and spirits up. We were flying with a total of seven A-10 units; later, a squadron of F-16s joined us for the war. Of the deployed A-10 units, the Black Panthers consistently kept the best maintenance statistics while outflying all but one other unit. That's teamwork! We were also privileged to have a great relationship with our pilots, especially the 353d TFS commander. When maintenance works with operations, everything goes much better. When the war started, we were prepared. Bunkers and aircraft-parking revetments were complete, we had a good aircraft flow plan with arm and dearm areas and hot pit refueling areas, and our integrated combat turn (ICT) teams were working together extremely well. During the war, we flew mostly Scud-hunting and search and destroy missions while using some aircraft for search and rescue (SAR) missions. We operated ICTs around the clock as we supported our night-flying sister squadron and reconfigured our aircraft for the next day's flying. We had regular Scud alarms, and from our bunkers we watched Scuds streak across the sky toward Dhahran or Riyadh. One hit near the end of our runway! We were comforted by a Patriot missile battery encamped near our flight line. Several aircraft were hit and damaged by enemy fire but were ably repaired by aircraft battle damage and repair teams deployed from depot. They even replaced an entire wing on one of our jets. Before the jet was repaired, we and other units cannibalized more than 200 parts from it. It's a miracle we were able to put it back together and fly it home with us. We lost two jets on one evening, but we got one of our pilots back after the war ended. We also supported two forward-operating locations near the Iraq border; we worked out a rotation schedule for all involved. When the ground war started, the weather turned bad and we were limited to SAR alert. By the time it cleared up, the war was over. We continued to maintain alert lines, but later began tearing down our base. We redeployed in mid-March—first in, first out.

Nightshift

by

Capt Lawrence M. Gatti

When the 4th Aircraft Maintenance Unit (AMU) of the 388th Tactical Fighter Wing (TFW) deployed to the Persian Gulf in August 1990, I expected a hot and tedious 90-day show-of-force TDY. I had just been assigned to the wing in June from a one-year remote tour in Korea. I really didn't expect the Iraqis to persist when a large US-led contingent arrived in-theater.

I was assistant OIC of the 4th AMU, and I worked the night shift for my OIC, Capt Jeff "Beaucoup" Moody. I was responsible for maintaining our twenty-four F-16C Block 40 Fighting Falcons. We were the first unit of the 388th TFW to arrive at the deployed location, and we were up and ready to fly within 24 hours. We spooled up to a normal daily flying training schedule and had settled into a routine within a week. The weather was miserably hot, so ensuring that my maintenance troops drank enough water was a primary concern during my nightly activities. After four and one-half months of rigid flying operations, my senses were considerably dulled. The deployment seemed more like a punishment than a mission of purpose, but the lethargy created by the endless training missions and seemingly meaningless alert commitments was abruptly shattered during the week of 13 January 1991.

While we knew that President Bush's deadline to the Iraqis was approaching, we hardly expected the order to cease training flights and begin loading a portion of our aircraft with live munitions. During the next few days, we discussed whether we would fight. The discussions ended dramatically. On 16 January, our assistant deputy commander for maintenance (DCM), Lieutenant Colonel Gilloth, called me to the DCM's office "immediately." I ran to the camouflaged trailer, where I was ushered to the table alongside the night shift supervisors of our sister AMUs, the 421st and the 69th. Emotionlessly, our DCM, Colonel Peterson, gave us the takeoff times, formations, and basic weapons loads for our first combat mission. While I heard the words, my mind was racing, thinking of the implications of our ensuing action. We had a chance to be a part of history, an important step in the changing face of the world.

After the briefing, I called my key supervisors together and asked them not to release the information until later in the night, as I had been ordered. We discussed weapons loading, fuzing, and aircraft launch procedures. Around midnight, I gathered the 90 members of the 4th AMU night shift into our hangar and briefed them on the start of combat operations.

Our first mission called for a large-force exercise (LFE) format, using 20 prime aircraft and four spares loaded with two mark-84, low-drag, general purpose, 2,000-pound bombs. The weapon load crews, crew chiefs, and systems specialists briskly double- and triple-checked their respective areas. Nobody wanted their aircraft left behind on the first combat mission. As the 0400 show time approached, several pilots filtered out of the operations trailers and walked to their aircraft. Some were subdued, some were animated, all were confident they could do their job. They visited with their crew chiefs and the other maintainers clustered around the aircraft.

I walked around each aircraft, questioning the crew chiefs about their jets and inspecting the aircraft and weapons. I spoke briefly to each of our pilots, shook their hands, and assured them they were taking the best aircraft in the Air Force into combat. They climbed into their cockpits, fired up their big GE turbofans, and checked their avionics and weapon systems. Several aircraft had problems that, though minor, required "redball" maintenance. (A redball is a problem occurring during launch which could impact mission capability.) All were rectified and the launch was going smoothly. I was riding in the "ramp rat" truck with the assistant operations officer, Major Collins.

We were at the end of the runway, looking over the running spare aircraft, when our wing commander's aircraft had a redball for inertial navigation unit (INU) battery failure. There were only 10 minutes

66

until launch, and the specialists worked furiously to replace the INU batteries in time for him to make the mission. As the technicians were finishing, Major Collins launched the sorties. He made the tough decision to send the first running spare in the wing commander's place. While unhappy about not being able to go on the first combat mission, the wing commander, Colonel Navarro, knew that a late takeoff could have jeopardized the mission. He approved the ramp rat's call.

As the last of the 20 Falcons climbed away into the purple-orange dawn, afterburners vibrated the ground. I realized how keyed up and anxious I had been. I felt exhausted but proud. The troops stood around bleary-eyed, staring into the morning sky—wishing, hoping, praying that all of their pilots and planes would return. I don't think sleep came easily to anyone that morning. I laid awake in my bunk, listening for the sound of 20 Falcons landing—and all 20 returned. Finally, I drifted to sleep. I awoke at 1600, anxious to see how our pilots did. I prepared for duty and went to the mess hall where many pilots loitered. I spotted one of my buddies, Lt Dan "Dawg" Swayne. He recounted the highlights of his mission and how pleased he was with his jet and its performance. I've never felt more proud of the men and women of the 4th AMU than at that moment.

The war lasted 43 days, and each day our pilots and aircraft completed missions and returned safely. Two aircraft were seriously damaged by SAM shrapnel and AAA fire, but both pilots landed their aircraft and escaped injury. Night after night, the 4th AMU worked 12-hour shifts, servicing, repairing, loading, and launching. They did this flawlessly and without complaint. I pushed them hard, and they responded like true professionals—the best of the best. As the war ended, we stepped down our alert status. Word filtered down that we would rotate back to Hill AFB on 18 April.

Our accomplishments were best summed up by Lieutenant Colonel Welsh, 4th Tactical Fighter Squadron (TFS) commander: "Over 1,000 combat sorties—*zero* major aircraft malfunctions over enemy territory. We can't repay that gift, but we'll never forget." I know I won't forget the contributions of these dedicated men and women.

Establishing a Forward Operating Location

by

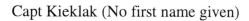

Capt Kieklak (No first name given)

On 5 January 1991, the 69th Tactical Fighter Squadron (TFS) deployed from Moody AFB, Georgia, to a base in the United Arab Emirates (UAE). Eleven days later, twelve F-16s from the 69 TFS took off on their first combat missions of Operation Desert Storm. A tremendous amount of work went into preparing the aircraft for the deployment, and an even greater effort was required to beddown and prepare for war operations. Still, both efforts paled in comparison to the task of moving the entire unit from the UAE to a forward operating location (FOL) in Saudi Arabia. This is an account of that move.

At about 0300 hours local, I was en route to the officer's compound after a 15-hour shift when the radio called me to Operations (Ops). I turned around and drove to the operations trailer, where I soon learned that the entire unit was deploying to King Fahd International Airport in Saudi Arabia. Four C-130s would be on the ramp in a matter of hours, and they would provide dedicated airlift for our supplies, equipment, and personnel. As the officer in charge of the 69th Aircraft Maintenance Unit (AMU), I was responsible for the twenty-four F-16s, 300 maintenance personnel, and all the support equipment associated with the unit. I immediately gathered my senior NCOs together and started working on a plan to move our whole operation north to King Fahd. Normally, deployment planning is handled by professional logisticians armed with computers. We planned the deployment with pencil, paper, coffee, and a pack of Dunhill cigarettes. Our plan wasn't pretty, but it would get us from point A to point B.

Soon, the C-130s arrived and we started loading our equipment and supplies. Since King Fahd had no F-16 support, we had to bring all of our equipment and personnel. The scene at the loading ramp was one of ceaseless activity: one airman referred to it as "controlled chaos." I deployed with the first load to arrange billeting and establish relations with the A-10 community. My first flight on a C-130 gave me an hour of much-needed sleep. I awoke with the first jolt of the C-130 touching down on the runway at King Fahd International Airport. The sheer vastness of the operation at King Fahd dwarfed any flight line I had seen. Soon a bus drove us to the huge tent city that housed the thousands of men and women stationed at King Fahd. Our arrival was anticipated, but there was no room at the inn. My troops were temporarily billeted in large "circus tents" that housed about 100. We grabbed a bite to eat at the finest chow hall in the area of responsibility (AOR), then we rode five miles from tent city to our corner of the flight line.

En route, we passed two solid miles of tarmac loaded with revetted A-10s. Everywhere I looked, I saw A-10s. We arrived at our ramp and began preparing for our aircraft. I left the NCOs in charge of setting up shop while I searched for the deputy commander for maintenance, Colonel Rupright. He and his commanders took great care of us. They gave us tents to work out of, revetments to shelter our aircraft and munitions, and much-needed vehicles. The maintenance operation center (MOC) provided us with radios and communications support. Assistance from the A-10 community was instrumental in helping us establish combat operations at King Fahd. By dusk, all of my troops were at King Fahd. While everyone was exhausted, there was no time for rest; our aircraft were flying their last missions out of the UAE and would soon be landing at King Fahd. The production superintendents and expediters developed a recovery and parking plan while the NCOIC worked with the flight chiefs on duty shifts and transportation arrangements. I went to Ops to find out about our next missions.

Our F-16s were equipped with low-altitude navigation and targeting infrared for night (LANTIRN) pods, which turned night into day. This capability made our unit the ideal choice for night missions, and that was why we were at King Fahd. We flew night missions and what we called "Scud-busting" duty. We flew 32 sorties the next night and anywhere from 35 to 45 sorties on the following nights. A week passed before we had our maintenance operation set up to our standards. Meanwhile, we generated sorties. Our first takeoffs were at sunset and the last two-ship was on the deck shortly after sunrise. We quickly adapted to our new environment, and we soon racked up an impressive record. In February, the 69th AMU generated 1,030 sorties.

We faced other challenges during our short tour in the AOR, but we all agreed that nothing was as challenging as the first 72 hours at King Fahd. Moving an entire AMU and TFS with literally no notice, then commencing full flying operations within 24 hours of establishing a FOL, was overwhelming.

What did I learn? First, while peacetime training goes a long way toward preparing us for war, we must always be ready to respond to the unexpected—for which there is no plan. Second, a lesson that company graders reflect upon after any successful operation: we can do nothing without the professionalism, hard work, and dedication of the enlisted corps. Their hard work was the foundation of Operation Desert Storm.

Geeks Go to War: Programming Under Fire

by

Capt Keith E. Kennedy

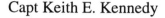

When you think of war, you think airplanes, tanks, pilots, artillery. When you think of Desert Storm, you probably think of Norman Schwarzkopf. So you're probably wondering what importance a computer programmer can have. What "major role" did I play? What did I do that made a difference?

I like to tell people, "I ran the war." Without me, the war would have come to a halt. Judging from the number of times I worked 24 or more hours straight, you'd think other people thought so too. Maybe you'll agree with me.

The story begins on the day Iraq invaded Kuwait. I was eight days away from graduating from Squadron Officer School. Suddenly, the tone of the lectures in the "Big Blue Bedroom" turned from budget cuts and force reductions to kicking butt. Several of my 800 classmates were immediately deployed to Southwest Asia, and several of my flight mates eventually made it to the war: a special operations chopper pilot, an RC-135 jock, a lawyer (yes, several jokes come to mind) and myself, a computer programmer.

When I returned home to Langley AFB, Virginia, the process of going to Saudi Arabia began. On three separate occasions I was told to pack up and go, and three times I didn't go. One of those times, I was within 24 hours of leaving the country. I flew to Bergstrom AFB, Texas, to deploy with the tactical air control center (TACC), not really knowing if I was actually going. When I got the word to go, I flew my wife and son down to say good-bye. The morning after they arrived, I was told not to go. Oh! ($600.00 down the drain.)

I finally left the US on 13 October 1990 on a VIP flight out of Andrews AFB and arrived in Riyadh, Saudi Arabia, on 14 October 1990.

No, I was not the VIP. The actor/comedian Steve Martin and his wife, Victoria Tennant, were our special guests. They were traveling to the area on a USO-sponsored trip to help boost our troops' morale.

For four years prior to Desert Storm, I was a software programmer, analyst, designer, and tester for the computer assisted force management system (CAFMS). This is the computer system that produced the air tasking order (ATO). I have read various publications that have not mentioned CAFMS and have given other computer systems such as TEMPLAR and FRAGWORKS credit for producing the ATO. Also, CAFMS has been the apparent "fall guy" for some of the communications problems associated with "delivering" the ATO to the Navy. Thus, it may not be politically acceptable to say what I'm about to say.

First, however, some background information: The tactical air war is planned and monitored at the TACC, a component of the tactical air control system (TACS). The TACC has two functional areas: combat plans and combat operations. In combat plans, preparing the daily ATO is an important, time-critical process. The ATO contains the mission and support data that flying units need. Combat operations is responsible for monitoring the missions as they are flown and making adjustments to the plans as the situation warrants.

TACC functions have been automated through a "modern" computerized tactical battle management system—CAFMS, the system I helped to develop and maintain while stationed at Langley AFB. CAFMS aids in preparing and disseminating the ATO. Additionally, CAFMS allows the TACC to constantly monitor the status of tactical resources such as aircrew, aircraft, and airfields through an array of tactical information displays. CAFMS also ties the TACC to its subordinate units—control and reporting centers (CRC), air support operations centers (ASOC), and wing operations centers (WOC, forward operating bases) through a near-real-time communication network. The system is configured as a star network with 20 local terminals located in both components of the TACC and 11 remote terminals located at the subordinate units. All the terminals, remote and local, are connected to a minicomputer that acts as the central node.

Combat plans prepares the daily ATO under this system. Simultaneously, information on the current tactical missions is continuously updated and monitored in combat operations. When the ATO is finished, the TACC notifies the remote sites and sends the ATO to their terminals, where it can be printed at the site printer. For those sites without a remote terminal, CAFMS can transmit the ATO directly over AUTODIN. The remote sites have full mission-monitoring and update capabilities. All terminals communicate with one another through an elaborate array of messages and formats.

Now, back to my part in the war: CAFMS was *the* computer system used during Operation Desert Shield/Storm to produce and disseminate the ATO and to monitor and update the war. As the war progressed, some problems arose. I deployed because I was one of the few CAFMS programmers left at Langley and because I had four years of experience with CAFMS.

Programming in the field is not a practice supported by many (if any) managers dealing with computer software development and maintenance. Nor is completely redesigning a *proven* hardware system. However, when the situation dictates, these things must be done.

During Desert Shield, CAFMS users identified several deficiencies in the computer system and several program problems that severely hampered day-to-day operations. The normal software development life cycle (SDLC), which includes lengthy design, coding, and testing times, was unacceptable to users in the area of responsibility (AOR) because the changes would have been completed after the war was over. The *only* acceptable solution was to deploy CAFMS programmers, with source code and all the necessary software in hand, to make modifications in the field.

MSgt Gary Boy was one of the other programmers at Langley who had the needed experience. So, armed with our "weapons," we jumped on an airplane and headed east. Sgt Kevin Rioles, a former member of the CAFMS programming team, had flown west from Osan AB, ROK, to help us when we arrived.

Programming in the field is not the best thing to try to do. First, in responding quickly to operational problems or system limitations, you lose analysis, design, and testing time (the critical part of the software development life cycle). The most important of these is testing. A programmer must ensure that all of the "bugs" are out of the software before it goes operational. Being "under the gun," we did not always have the luxury of time. Second, the pristine environment of a software support facility gives the programmer the proper conditions to carefully analyze program problems and make complex software modifications. By proper conditions, I mean a single, dedicated machine on which to modify programs. Conditions in the field, during exercises and especially during Desert Shield/Storm, were never pristine. Third, configuring software is difficult at best. Balancing software that is currently running on an operational system with software that is changing is a full-time job. When there is only one computer system to contend with, the job is tough. Throw in four more, and it becomes a nightmare. But, given the situation, we had to do our best.

When we arrived in Saudi Arabia, we went right to work. Since time was of the essence, we had to identify all system problems and propose enhancements quickly. Fortunately, we already had over 20 requests from the first two and one-half months of Desert Shield. Next, we had to prioritize these changes. Key personnel from both combat plans and combat operations met to help us prioritize these changes. During peacetime, this process can take six months or more—considering the time to gather all the change requests, formalize these requests, and bring together all the users to create a prioritized list. During Desert Shield, all the affected personnel were right there, and they quickly agreed on a prioritized list of changes. The process only took a week.

During this time, I performed some initial analysis and design. We cut a majority of the up-front time, leaving more time for actual coding and testing.

Another limitation usually associated with programming in the field is not having a dedicated computer system (the pristine environment). The CAFMS computer system overcomes this obstacle because each CAFMS "system" contains two complete computers, providing an immediate backup should one computer fail. As an added feature, terminals can be switched to the second computer with the touch of a button. During "slow" periods of the war, usually at night, we would turn on the second computer, boot up our development system, switchover three to five terminals, and begin fixing problems. Since there were five complete systems in the AOR, we had five systems at our disposal.

My biggest headache was configuration management of these five computer systems. By the end of my deployment, 13 March 1991, some 80 problems and enhancements had been identified. I was responsible for (1) ensuring all changes were documented, no matter how minor; (2) ensuring all changes and enhancements were properly and adequately tested; and (3) ensuring the changes were properly installed on all five computers. This was not any easy task. As much as I don't like the documentation aspect of software development, however, this was important because all the changes we made during the war had to be integrated into the baseline software back at Langley. Additionally, my boss, Colonel Witt, USCENTAF/SC, expressed his concern for keeping documentation.

What we did, from the user's perspective, was nothing short of amazing. (Yes, I'm patting my own back.) I made 90 percent of the software changes myself. At one time or another, I touched each and every one of the 150-plus separate software program modules in CAFMS. My two "compadres," Master Sergeant Boy and Sergeant Rioles, were a BIG help. The procedure discussed below was their idea—they designed it, they did most of the programming and hardware modifications themselves, they spent the long, 20-plus-hour days supporting the system in the time that followed.

Software problems weren't the only reason we were there. As the US forces began to build in the area, General Horner, USCENTAF commander, realized that 31 terminals (20 local and 11 remotes) were not enough, but hardware limitations kept us from increasing the number of terminals. So, in September 1990, an additional CAFMS computer was deployed. In November 1990, yet another full CAFMS complement was brought in, bringing the total number of CAFMS-accessible terminals to 60 locals and 33 remotes.

Now we had three CAFMS computers, all located within 30 feet of each other, 60 local terminals spread throughout the TACC, and 33 remote terminals scattered over Southwest Asia. But the three separate computers were just that—separate. Information could not be easily passed from CAFMS to CAFMS. The ATO information was transferred via the reliable "tennis shoe interface." Mission information was copied onto a removable disk pack and hand-carried to the other CAFMS systems. With just three CAFMS systems, this process was moderately time consuming. But with two more CAFMS systems, which arrived around New Year's, an information management nightmare came to life.

And that was just half the problem. Combat operations personnel, depending on which of the five CAFMS they were connected to, might only see one-fifth of the needed mission information. Daily reports had to be assembled from the separate systems and manually collated into a usable document. This too was a time-consuming process.

The solution was a network. But we could not just insert communication boards to facilitate network communications, and we could not buy additional cables and other hardware. In fact, nothing was available on the market, either in Saudi Arabia or the US, to help us.

To implement this network, we used existing hardware and software to create the CAFMS network database management system. Three areas within the software had to be modified or created: applications software, memory management, and communications software between the systems.

My area of responsibility was the user application software, the software which runs behind what is seen on the screen by the user. I concentrated on the programs used by combat operations, since this data was the only information not easily accessible to all users. I modified each of the combat operations-oriented programs to initiate the transfer of data between machines. This was a simple (but tedious) process because I had to thoroughly analyze each program and identify the "correct" data transfer points. The hard part was I had to modify our data base structure to accommodate an "easy" update of data records.

Master Sergeant Boy handled the most critical part of the software network, the memory management software. Probably the best feature was "store and forward," the capability to store data in the event communications were lost to any of the other four computers. We stored the data on disk to insure against any of the other computers being down. Storing the data before actually passing it also helped prevent data loss, should the computer passing the information go down.

Sergeant Rioles completely engineered the communications software. All necessary communications were handled by writing the software in assembler (bits and bytes). The big area of concern was detecting loss of communications to another computer. Eventually, all the individual CAFMS systems talked to each other, knew when they weren't talking, and, in most cases, knew exactly why they weren't talking.

But software was only part of the network. The hardware completed the project. We used the existing hardware and cables to physically connect the computers. Since the local terminals were connected to CAFMS using fiber-optic cables to individual ports, we stole five ports (five terminals) from each computer and physically connected the five systems. Each CAFMS computer was connected to the other four through short sections of fiber optic cable. This allowed a simultaneous transfer of data to all connected computers. Within nanoseconds, an update made to CAFMS would show on all four other CAFMS.

Each CAFMS contained four 80-megabyte (MB) disk drives, with removable disk packs. (This was how the ATO data was transferred between systems.) But as the war progressed, 320 MB per system was insufficient. We could only store two days of combat operation mission data (yesterday's and today's) and three days of combat plans data (yesterday's, today's, and tomorrow's). All this data, plus the additional resources data, would not fit. Back at Langley, 20 new disk drives were researched, evaluated, and purchased to boost the CAFMS storage capability. Within approximately one week, we had installed the disk drives and transferred all the software and data—with only 10 minutes downtime to reboot the computer. With the additional two disk drives per CAFMS, the storage capacity was boosted from 320 MB to 1,200 MB (1.2 gigabytes).

Ok, I know what you're thinking! "Throw three software geeks together with nothing else to do and anything can be done." While this statement is true, the real significance of this is that the network was completed, from idea to implementation, in just over one month. In fact, we were up and running in early January, just days before the war started.

Why do I say, "I ran the war"? There are two reasons. Imagine what would have happened if CAFMS went down. Could you have produced a 100+ section ATO in one day and put it in the hands of literally hundreds of Navy, Army, Marine, and Air Force personnel within an hour? I ran the war. Second, General Horner referred to the ATO as "a single sheet of music from which everybody played." In the grand symphony that was Desert Storm, CAFMS produced the score, and I was one of the composers and conductors. I ran the war.

Public Affairs Liaison for Military Airlift Command

by

Capt Doug Kinneard

Hurlburt Field, Florida—I was a 1st lieutenant in the public affairs (PA) office under the 1st Special Operations Wing (1st SOW) when Operation Desert Shield kicked off. Initially, our policy statement to dozens of news reporters who called regularly was, "I'm sorry; it's our policy not to discuss any deployment of forces either in real world contingency or exercise scenarios. We cannot confirm or deny 1st SOW involvement in the Gulf region."

There were, however, nonspecial operations units and people from Hurlburt going to Saudi Arabia whose missions we could talk about—for example, the Air Force Special Operations School's (USAFSOS) mid-east culture course instructors. They put together briefings to prepare thousands of deploying military members for the cultural, religious, and political milieu they could expect in the Gulf. I escorted news reporters on base for interviews with USAFSOS instructors. We allowed some civil engineer troops who had returned early from Saudi to talk to the media about setting up tent cities and building up bases over there.

Because 1st SOW public affairs was not programmed for a mobility position, it never occurred to me that I could be sent to Saudi. But when the Military Airlift Command public affairs (MAC/PA) director asked about sending an officer over on a special mission, my supervisor answered, "Oh, Kinneard, yeah, he's raring to go over there." That was true. I had expressed in no uncertain terms that I was willing to deploy if someone were needed from our office.

"We need someone to go into Dhahran where the Joint Information Bureau (JIB) is set up, to act as an independent MAC liaison between

81

them and the Saudi information bureau," the MAC/PA deputy director explained.

I was nominated in September to go in mid-October. I remember feelings of excitement at this great opportunity and feelings of apprehension at leaving my wife and three young children.

"You will sponsor, host, and direct MAC's flying in civilian news teams from hometowns all over the US. You will help them get the strategic and tactical airlift story," the lieutenant colonel said. "You'd be in there, hopefully, only 90 days, and since you'll be working directly for CINCMAC, I'll do everything I can to pull you out before the shooting starts."

I felt qualified to do the job, since much of my PA experience had been working with news reporters. I had escorted national news media personnel at Hurlburt Field for stories about special operations and for two international airlift competitions (Airlift Rodeo) at Pope AFB, North Carolina. I had even provided media assistance during a presidential visit and a Bob Hope television show taped with an Air Force audience and USAF aircraft as the stage setting. I never imagined this new assignment would include close work with both a US president and Bob Hope.

For this former Boy Scout and camping enthusiast, the novelty and adventure of going to the desert were good compensation for any fear of danger or thought of not returning. I drew a box of "Meals Ready to Eat," and I loved every one of them. I borrowed a shoulder holster and scrounged other holsters because I was forewarned of the shortage of these items in Saudi. The SMSgt who worked with me in Saudi traded these and other items for much-needed canteens and miscellaneous items.

This seasoned 20-year NCO proved himself most adept in the people and supply businesses. He immediately procured two vehicles that were very appropriate for our unique mission requirements: a new Nissan 7-passenger van and a new Toyota sedan. These were essential for transporting the 5-member news teams that arrived every three or four days for their news-gathering tours.

I arrived at the King Abdul Azziz Airport on 16 October and took a bunk in a Saudi military dormitory on an adjacent base. My room had

11 other USAF members sleeping in it throughout the day and night, so the lights were always off and the air conditioning was always on. It was actually cold in there, and I used the heavy arctic sleeping bag on the twin bed assigned to me. The bed had a mattress which slouched so badly that I soon supported it with a piece of plywood scrounged from a nearby carpenter's shop. We were very grateful for such luxury accommodations after witnessing some of our comrades' living conditions. The Saudi dorm had hot showers, indoor toilets (although the Arab-style toilet holes on the floor took some getting used to), and sinks and mirrors.

On the day I arrived, I met my partner and some of the public affairs people working the JIB at the Dhahran International Hotel, six miles away. Our first media group arrived the next day. They landed at Dhahran and taxied up to a flight line managed by MAC's 438th airlift control element (ALCE). The first group was from New Jersey—the same area the ALCE deployed from. The reporters were satisfied walking along the ramp and interviewing mechanics, crew chiefs, transportation officers, and ALCE members who operated the mini-command post on the airfield.

Many 16-hour days in the sunshine were broken up by driving the reporters to lunch in Dhahran, Kobar, or one of the six messing facilities on base (where they continued to interview and take pictures). We also allowed them to visit the JIB, and some reporters took side trips off the compound to British or American marine camps. We took others to King Fahd Airport, about an hour north, to visit A-10 squadrons based there. The variety and scope of story ideas and photo opportunities we provided the visiting reporters seemed to meet their needs. Each news media group consisted of two or three news reporters and one or two escorting PA officers or NCOs. Some wanted to visit downtown areas, so we arranged a Saudi escort. We prepared for, met, and cared for these reporters while they were there, and we put them on a MAC transport plane back to the States after two days.

On many occasions, reporters would write or fax a request in advance. They asked us to find specific people or units for them to meet and interview, usually people whose families they had already interviewed back home. We kept busy between groups finding these contacts and setting up itineraries. In contrast to the negative publicity generated later, when "media pools" were established, the MAC-sponsored reporters we hosted were all very satisfied with the stories and access we arranged for them. Many even sent stories, photos, and thank-you letters after they returned to the US. Some won awards for their work.

In my liaison duties, I assisted the Central Command JIB in many ways. As the key MAC/PA officer, I had close ties to the flight line. I arranged for taping Willard Scott's weather show from one of our C-5s (he wore a MAC baseball cap while on the air). I also met, worked with, or escorted, Jay Leno, Steve Martin, Tommy Hearns, and O. J. Simpson.

Activities on the Dhahran flight line were sometimes the only news-gathering opportunities available to JIB reporters, especially during holidays. By Christmas, our leaders felt that those who had deployed there with no notice and had not heard any word about rotation deserved a break from news interviews. Consequently, news interviews were canceled for the holidays.

I also worked with some reporters who were not flown into the country on MAC aircraft on 48-hour special visas: Dan Rather and reporters from the Discovery Channel, the *Christian Science Monitor,* and *Aviation Week.* Hundreds of reporters stayed at the now famous Dhahran Hotel where the JIB was, so my efforts were trivial compared to the courtesies and privileges extended to me by the JIB. They provided contacts in the field, phones, fax machines, restaurant privileges, and convenience. The JIB enabled us to arrange the hometown news media tours, and we got the airlift story out in a big way. It was an effective program for MAC.

The excitement during Thanksgiving Day was hard to match, since President George Bush and some congressmen were on our ramp for speeches and photo opportunities. I assisted some 300 White House Press Corps reporters and 300 JIB reporters as they traveled northward to cover the President's Thanksgiving meals with Marine units.

I enjoyed Christmas. The new master sergeant working for me played Santa Claus for a family who invited us to Christmas Eve dinner at the Aramco base (a compound comprised of US civilians working for Saudi Arabia). On Christmas day we met Bob Hope, Johnny Bench, and Aaron Tippin (country musician) at a USO news conference. The MAC/PA director who escorted them arranged for a press conference where Johnny Bench and Bob Hope pinned my captain's bars on me. It was a surprise and a very memorable photo opportunity. Thanks, MAC/PA! I then took the entourage on a tour through an AC-130 gunship with my wing commander at his deployed site. During the taping of the USO show Christmas night, we met the celebrities backstage at the King Fahd hangar. NBC aired the show on 12 January, the day I returned home.

At my PA director's suggestion, I used my special orders to hop some tactical airlift missions and tour the area of responsibility between Christmas and New Year's Day. Since no media was due in that week, I visited PAs who were deployed with their units to determine which areas could host news media groups. It also enabled me to buoy up PA specialists who were working very hard in secluded

Celebrities All

85

areas, under austere conditions. I spent one or two days at each of five bases scattered around the Arabian Peninsula. One area host took me snorkeling on New Year's Day in the Gulf of Oman. (Their lobster are like our Florida spiny lobsters; we saw them in only six feet of water!)

On New Year's Day, we sponsored a few more hometown media groups flown in by MAC. The CENTCOM commander canceled our program in early January 1991, and MAC followed through on its promise to withdraw me. I left the AOR on 12 January, four days before the air war began.

I gained much from my 90-day experience in Saudi Arabia during Desert Shield. I met Dan Rather, Peter Jennings, Tom Brokaw, CNN's Christiane Amanpour, and Geraldo Rivera, as well as dozens of other professional journalists from all around America and Europe. These contacts helped me to build up a network of professional affiliations that I value. As a result, two of the media organizations I worked with in Saudi have visited Hurlburt since I returned.

The Discovery Channel produced a piece about AC-130 gunships that aired on their "Firepower" series. New York City's WABC television station broadcast live from Hurlburt three days in a row. They focused on issues related to terrorism and the USAFSOS instruction there.

I also had faith-promoting religious experiences over there, which I have shared with others. My duties enabled me and the two NCOs who worked with me to interact extensively with both Saudi and Kuwaiti nationals, and to learn much about them and their rich Arab culture and heritage. My family also grew immensely from my experience in Saudi through the regular letters I sent packed with interesting information. I filled a journal with observations and details about history in the making. I have a good portfolio of stories and photos that I assisted journalists in publishing, and I gave an interview to my own hometown news media by telephone on Christmas Day.

I felt particularly blessed during my Desert Shield experience. Soon after returning, I attended SOS in residence and traded many stories with other captains who served over there. From what I gathered, many positive, uplifting experiences have resulted from the conflict in Southwest Asia. My own memoirs will serve as personal adventures and anecdotes in our family story times. I'm thankful for the trust placed in me and the responsibility given to me to represent Military Airlift Command as its spokesman and in-country liaison during that historical period.

An Officer First

by

Capt Roseanne Warner

"Roseanne, the war started." I thought I was dreaming, since it was before dawn. But Phil, my husband, had been watching the news. Right then, I had a dreadful feeling. It's hard to describe. I prepared, knowing the recall would come, and it came like clockwork. I remember looking at Becca, my little girl, and trying to memorize every little detail about her sleeping body. Wondering when I would see her again tore at my heart. Would she understand why her mommy was going away? Phil and I had been through the usual military separations and were better prepared to handle it, or so I thought. I drove to work thinking the night was particularly dark.

The clinic was brightly lit and bustling with activity. We had prepared a 500-bed contingency hospital for Desert Storm. While we waited for our deployment orders, we got our real-world chemical gear, shots, and last-minute administrative stuff. Phil met me after dropping Becca off at preschool. It was emotional.

Since we were a small clinic and they needed nurses, I went to Wiesbaden Hospital by myself. On the way there, I felt very alone and scared. I thought about the possible types of injuries, and I was glad for all of the combat casualty care course (C^4) medical readiness training I had received. It was a tough course, but I felt good when I completed it because it pushed me to do things I hadn't done before. I thought about all the chemical warfare training we had received in the NATO tac evaluations at Zweibrucken, and it became very close and personal. I was confident I could don my gear in an attack and stay in it for hours. I didn't have that kind of intense training until I arrived in Europe.

89

The security police at Wiesbaden were on alert, checking each car underneath with mirrors and pulling them over to look in trunks. I finally found a parking slot, then the chief nurse's office. She tried to put us at ease. She had one of those dress mannequins in her office with her BDU shirt on it, a brown bag made to look like a face with big red lips, and a hat on top. She said it was a target for the terrorists! They were getting bomb threats from antiwar people. How do you evacuate a 500-bed hospital at all, especially without chaos?

I met other nurses in the "same boat" as me—out of our old units. We sat together and got our duties. When we found our rooms, I was amazingly tired. We toured the huge place and met the people we would be working with the next day. I went back and watched Armed Forces Network (AFN) before sleeping.

Although I'm an OB/GYN practitioner, I was on an orthopedic floor. I was overwhelmed in that environment, but I quickly returned to the basics because of the sense of urgency to learn before the rush of patients. The crew on 3E was a good bunch, and I'll always remember the feeling of togetherness. Major "T" (Tubbiolo) was a strong charge nurse and a good leader. She always seemed to hold it together. I read all I could about inner strength, peace, faith. I thought about all the courses I had in leadership. I thought about all the young technicians on the floor. I wanted to be a good example for them. They were getting on-the-job training in a big way. I thought about all the time we had practiced with casualties in our "med red" exercises and the things I had done when in charge of the casualty collection point (CCP). I had worked hard to keep morale high in the midst of confusion and waiting. We were a team, and each of us was an important link to getting the job done. When I was in charge, I drew on every experience in my life to get people moving. I never realized how important each leadership event is in our lives, or how important it is to be part of a team.

Several of my patients had Purple Hearts. One patient was in the Scud missile attack in Dhahran. A couple of his friends were killed, and he was in shock. I cared for shrapnel, gunshot, and mortar wounds. I cared for all branches—Army, Navy, Marines, and Air Force. One marine with a Purple Heart said, "If anybody ever says they weren't scared, they're liars—I was scared to death. All of a sudden there were 100 Iraqi tanks pointed at us, and thank God for the Air Force! We radioed and the A-10s came and bombed the hell out them. You see, we were a forward unit and the artillery was behind us. They still managed to hit us—that's how I was wounded."

I'll never forget the faces—some just stay with me. I was glad there was American support for these guys back home, because whether the antiwar protesters liked it or not, these guys were the reason they had the right to protest and the freedom of speech to say horrible things. I thought how awful it must have been for the Vietnam veterans to come back from a horrible ordeal to their own people spitting on them. I saw some bad injuries that made it hard to deal with the war machine, but these patients needed me. I dealt with the clinical aspects of war instead of the other issues. We all rationalize every day. Soldiers, airmen, and seamen have to do this or they can't function. Some amputees cried when I changed their dressings because it was horribly painful, but I had to convince myself I was hurting them to make them better. Many times I cried too, but I continued on and seemed to get through each day.

I sat and talked with the guys when I had a break. One fell 30 feet off a berm on the Iraqi border at night. He lay there with his possibly broken back for one and one-half hours in the dark with the enemy nearby. He finally shot off his flare and prayed that the ones who came for him would be friendly. He was lucky. Another soldier came down from a chopper by rope with a 100-pound pack on his back. He fell straight down, compressing his spinal cord. The survivor of the Chinook chopper crash was still dazed when we got him. He was in traction. Another stepped on a land mine and had his feet blown up. His dressing changes were intense. He screamed at the Iraqis to focus his pain.

One day I could watch the TV no longer. I was oversaturated with war news. I didn't want to read the *Stars and Stripes* any more. That cut off some of the baggage and made it easier. I missed Phil and Becca, and I knew she was having a hard time at preschool. The teachers tried to fill in with extra attention. The first night I was back home, she lay on my stomach with her arms tight around my neck all night, as if holding me back from going anywhere. I missed her third birthday, and Phil's birthday too. Her fourth was a big party—my way of making up for the one that got away.

When I returned to Zweibrucken, I felt out of sync with everything. It was like "well we had the war and now what is my function?" We had built up for so many months, and we had carried out our roles like we had always trained. Somehow, coming back seemed deflated. The "ordinary" jobs had less significance somehow. Nevertheless, when we left Germany in April 1991, I felt relieved. Becca had her little American flag ready to wave. We arrived in Charleston that evening. I don't know what happened, but the feeling was patriotism. There were yellow ribbons everywhere! A sea of yellow, and Becca was saying, "This is America, Mommy—America!" I felt proud to have played a part and made a difference in these men's lives. I felt peace.

The war affected me in ways that I've only recently realized. I think I'm less naive, even more passionate in my causes, acutely aware of time, impatient with rework, and frustrated when I can't motivate others to think like I think they should. I am thankful for an opportunity to share my experiences with others and to share in the experiences of others. Why do I stay? Because it's an honor, and it's my responsibility to be the best officer I can be in this force. I will make a difference in the lives of other officers and uphold the traditions to which I am bound.

Tactical Deception in the Desert—Scathe Mean

by

Capt Phil Smith

For me, the Desert Shield/Storm experience was the culmination of four years of training. I received that training while assigned as a ground launched cruise missile (GLCM) flight commander at Comiso AB, Sicily, and at Davis-Monthan AFB, Arizona. The GLCM part of the equation is significant because my mission employed many of the operational concepts previously used in the recently inactivated ground launched cruise missile system. These concepts include convoy operations, perimeter ground defense, land navigation, field living, self-aid/buddy care, and nuclear, biological, and chemical (NBC) skills. My mission, code-named "Scathe Mean," specifically involved launching Northrop BQM-74 aerial target drones into key target areas in Iraq. I'll describe the history behind the mission, the training of my team, and the execution of the mission.

Pentagon air planners were very concerned about the air defense net that was located all across Iraq. This air defense system consisted of Soviet, British, and US radars and missiles linked together through the sophisticated French-built Kari command, control, and communications system. For coalition air power to successfully strike key targets, we needed a method of breaking through the defense system, destroying these targets, and minimizing loss of airframes and pilots. Operation Scathe Mean evolved as a way to lure Iraqi radar systems into revealing themselves so that our high-speed anti-radiation missiles (HARM) fired from F-4G Wild Weasels, F/A-18s, and EA-6Bs could destroy them. My job was to launch drones, which generated a radar signature similar to allied fighter/bombers, ahead of the initial air strikes into Iraq. These drones looked like a short version of a cruise missile. I became involved in September 1990, under a shroud of secrecy.

I was notified on 24 September 1990 that I'd been selected to perform a classified mission. I was to report to a location in California on 26 September 1990. During the 24 hours prior to my departure, my mind ran through all sorts of possibilities. After all, I had been involved with a tactical nuclear system just two months earlier. With an accompanying increase in heart rate, I thought the unthinkable. All became crystal clear when I arrived in California and was briefed into the mission.

I have vivid recollections of my old boss from the GLCM training group at Davis-Monthan AFB, Col Robert Livingston, escorting me into the briefing room. A Pentagon air planner told us that two flights of Air Force personnel would form and train to launch BQM-74 aerial target drones. These flights would consist of personnel from varying Air Force specialty codes (AFSC), including security police, vehicle maintenance, aerospace ground equipment, avionics, communications, missile maintenance, explosive ordnance, and independent duty medical technicians. Only 50 percent of the men had experience and training in ground combat skills.

Once trained, we would fly into King Khalid Military City (KKMC), approximately 50 miles from the Iraqi border. At KKMC we would billet with Army Special Forces and continue to train until called upon to go to war. Once notified, my flight was to drive approximately 350 miles to a remote location and wait until dark. Then, using night vision goggles (NVG), drive into the desert and configure our equipment for launch. At the designated hour, we were to launch drones into Baghdad and the H-2 and H-3 airfields located in western Iraq. We were to stay in position and continue to launch through the following two days in support of follow-on strikes.

I became concerned about staying in a fixed position for an extended period of time because we would create a large noise and light signature which could be seen for miles in the desert. I requested a "shoot and move" strategy to complicate enemy targeting. I received approval and filed away the fact that I'd need to survey several sites once I arrived in-theater. Now began the challenge of training my team.

Training for Scathe Mean occurred in two distinct phases. The first phase, and priority number one for mission accomplishment, was learning how to set up and launch the target drones. The second phase, of real concern to me, was basic combat survival skills. The first phase of training took place in California and lasted for 10 days. During that time, we drilled extensively on the checklists and equipment necessary to get the drones in the air—drones that had never been launched by Air Force personnel before. This was done through repetition of hands-on experience with the equipment. Essentially, what we had to do was take a fully fueled drone from a crate and place it on a launch rail. Then we had to attach the wings for rocket boost off the launch rail. Once assembled, we simply connected power and erected the drone into launch position.

We were able to practice only basic procedures, and many of our actions were simulated because we could not actually launch drones. Also, we couldn't use the large cranes we'd be using in the field because we were training in limited space . . . indoors. Additionally, when we did this for real, it would be at night with no moon illumination. To simulate night operations, we turned the lights out in the training area and practiced with red-lensed flashlights. At the end of the training period in California, we assembled all of the basic equipment and supplies we needed, became proficient in basic launch procedures, did some rudimentary combat skills training, and got to know one another a little better. Many of our supplies (camping stoves, compasses, canteens) were purchased on the local economy at places like Kmart or Sam's Club because we had to prepare quickly. I still needed to train the troops in a number of different areas, but that would have to wait until we were in-theater. On 6 November 1990, we boarded three C-5 Galaxies and began the long trip to Saudi Arabia.

We arrived at KKMC on 7 November 1990. I recall climbing down the ladder into the cargo hold and watching the cargo door open to a surrealistic scene. Flat, rocky desert with the sun beating down. The air shimmered because ground temperature was already 95°F at 0830 hours. I remember thinking, "This is it, it's time to get to work." The first order of business was to deplane the troops and gear, stow the gear, and get the troops settled in. We were fortunate in that we'd come prepared to live in tents but were billeted in fairly new dormitories. We had indoor plumbing, regular beds, and two hot meals a day provided by Army Special Forces units and the Saudi government. At least my men wouldn't have to worry about living conditions.

We worked nonstop the first 30 days. We started at dawn and returned to the dorm after dark. Our days consisted of inventory, inspection, checkout, and repair of equipment and vehicles. Additionally, we went out at least twice a week for field training. During these field training sessions, we practiced convoy speed and spacing as well as land navigation and site roll-on techniques. We were finally able to fully employ all of our large vehicles, including the cranes, and drone setup time for launch fell from nine hours to three.

By the first week in December, we were sure we would be in Saudi Arabia for a while. The troops were becoming frustrated, and I decided to put them on a regular training schedule that would include one day off per week. I could see some symptoms of "burnout," so I figured the best way to help overcome it was to publish a schedule of events one week in advance. That way, the men could plan ahead a little and get some kind of order into their lives. We conducted physical training, which included stretching, push-ups, sit-ups, and a two-mile run, three times a week at 0630. I knew the troops must be in good condition to deal with physical and emotional stress. I also began to focus my team on some of the detail work necessary for field survival.

I felt it important that each member of my flight possess rudimentary desert navigation skills because key leaders could be incapacitated by on-site or convoy attack. To that end, I took a civilian road atlas, which was available at local book stores, and manufactured route folders for each vehicle. In much the same way "AAA" does with their "Tripkits," I photocopied interconnecting maps and highlighted the route we were to follow. These folders would allow the men to approximate their position and proceed to major roadways should they have to retrograde through the desert. Additionally, all of my troops became proficient in using the global positioning system (GPS) equipment. This equipment told the troops on the ground their latitude and longitude by electronically syncing with global positioning satellites. I put my men in vehicles and had them navigate through a presurveyed course, finding known checkpoints with the GPS, to increase their proficiency in land navigation.

Another major concern was basic weapon proficiency. Sure, it helps to shoot straight, but did the men understand how to employ their weapons in a firefight? I took a twofold approach to solving this problem. First, we took the troops out to the firing range at KKMC. At the range, the men were able to put some rounds through their M-16s to make sure that the weapon functioned properly and that they could hit the target. Sounds basic, right? Remember, many of my troops were working in the vehicle repair shop on the flight line at Davis-Monthan only six weeks earlier. How many of you have gone to the range recently? How about field stripping and cleaning the weapon? These were common problems for us. For example, when I picked up my weapon from the mobility armory, it had never been lubricated or fired before. So, weapons-firing became a priority.

A more complicated problem was that of training the troops in firefight procedures should the convoy be ambushed—and 325 miles there and back is a long way. With this in mind, we undertook the second phase of weapons training: convoy ambush procedures. We had 17 vehicles in the convoy. I led in a Chevy Blazer with my lead security policeman, MSgt Tony Gross. Behind me was a four-man fire team in a high-mobility multi-purpose wheeled vehicle (HMMWV). Two additional fire teams were interspersed throughout the convoy, while the fourth fire team brought up the trail position. The fire teams were armed with M-60 machine guns, M-203 grenade launchers, M-16s, and fragmentary grenades. Each maintenance technician in the remaining vehicles carried an M-16.

We were strictly defensive in nature. Our plan, if hit, was to keep moving and live to fight another day. In the worst case, our avenue of escape could become blocked and we would have to stand and fight. We spent many hours in the desert doing simulated attacks, training for that worst case. The security police practiced moving their HMMWVs into position to lay down a base of fire with the heavy weapons (M-60s, M-203s) while my maintenance technicians learned to support them from the rear, close in to the convoy, and not shoot them in the back. All of these scenarios were done dry-fire, but at least the troops were exposed to a basic plan; we'd have a chance should trouble come.

The chemical threat was another major concern. Chemicals added to the training burden and to troop anxiety. We spent at least one session per week reviewing basic procedures like auto injector usage, mask donning and clearing drills, and field-expedient decontamination procedures. We coupled this with self-aid/buddy-care techniques by putting the troops through scenarios that included simulated combat injuries ranging from treating shock to setting an intravenous line.

Along with the above training, I went out on the road to survey several launch sites. I was able to assess the predominant terrain features (typically flat), driving conditions, and soil stability. I made several trips down our convoy route, logging exact mileage information and documenting checkpoints with the GPS. I took my largest six-wheel-drive crane with me to ensure we'd have no problem with large trucks off the road in the sand. The truck I'd selected, although the heaviest, had the best "footprint" in terms of weight distribution. This factored in heavily when we actually performed the mission.

We had a green light for the mission at 2300 on 15 January 1991. Since most of the troops were already in the rack, we decided not to alert them right away so they could get some rest. I busied myself with final preparations, which included checks on radio frequencies, sign/countersign procedures, and the current threat analysis. At 0300 we woke the troops, and told them an "H" hour had been established. We would launch at approximately 0300 the following morning, 17 January 1991.

Everyone assembled downstairs in the dorm. At 0345 I stood before the troops and gave them the operations order. The realization that this was what we had been training for sank in very quickly. Reality hits you square in the face when you slap a clip of .556 ammo into your weapon and ingest your first bromide tablet to counteract the effects of nerve agent. As I looked out at the 43 men assembled in front of me, I could see a wide range of human emotion looking back: apprehension, excitement, relief that the wait was over. Then the training, professionalism, and pure volume of things we had to do took over. After transitioning to our storage hangar, we began assembling the vehicles into convoy formation.

While my maintenance superintendent, SMSgt Van Bertram, took care of the vehicle marshaling, I got the current weather from the forecasters. At 0530, I led the first half of my convoy across the base and out the main gate. We split the convoy up as we traversed the base so as not to draw attention to ourselves. The remaining half of the convoy joined us about three miles off base, and our long journey began.

The route we followed was simple, but it passed through some high-threat areas. We headed north from KKMC to Hafar Al Batin, a small town known to contain many Iraqi sympathizers. We felt this was a place for a potential compromise of our convoy, so we kept a wary eye out, especially to the rear to ensure that we weren't being followed. To make us appear less threatening, we did not mount any of the M-60 machine guns in the HMMWV turrets. Finally, we traveled "communication out" so the Iraqis could not intercept any of our radio signals.

From Hafar Al Batin, we proceeded west through Rafhah to a point just east of Arar. We traveled a two-lane highway that paralleled an above-ground oil pipeline. During the trip, I fell back through the convoy periodically to check for load shifting, driver fatigue, and potential air or ground threats. At 1700, after 11 hours of driving, I stopped the convoy about 15 miles short of the launch site. I then took one of the interspersed fire teams and drove to the site so they could secure the area while I went back for the rest of the flight. At 1900 I rolled the flight off the improved road and into the desert. I told everyone to pull the fuses that controlled the brake lights and headlights on the big trucks, so lights wouldn't work. We then waited for darkness.

At nightfall, we put on our NVGs and began the slow roll into the desert. Although I had been out to the site only two hours earlier, I couldn't navigate without the GPS. Imagine trying to find a spot in the desert with no moon illumination and no visible landmarks. I simply followed the directions of my lead defender, Sergeant Gross, as he monitored the GPS system and told me how to steer our vehicle.

At the site, I quickly dismounted and began positioning the other vehicles so we could prepare to launch. I parked the two trucks

99

carrying the air compressors and portable power generators at site center. We spaced these trucks about 10 feet apart, parallel to one another, so I could launch the drones from either side of them. I then began pacing the distances to the points where the launchers went. I marked each spot with a "glow stick" so each driver would know the relative layout of the site and be able to maneuver his vehicle accordingly. None of this was simple because NVGs take away most of your peripheral vision and depth perception.

The final site layout was a straight line of launchers on each side of the centrally located compressor vehicles. I thought we were ready to set the equipment up, but as the vehicles moved into position to off-load the launchers and drones, things went wrong. Five of the large flatbed trucks bogged down in the sand. Although I took the heaviest vehicle onto this site to test the soil composition, I didn't realize the other trucks would cut through the top four to six inches of hard-packed sand and dig into the loose sand below. Here we were, stuck in the sand, with our launch window rapidly approaching. Talk about the friction of war! All we could do was lighten the load on each vehicle by taking the equipment off. We would worry about moving the trucks later.

I had the large crane move into position and lift the launchers to the ground. Then, 12 to 14 men carried them to their proper positions. Next, each fully fueled 500-pound drone was lowered into our waiting arms and carried to the launchers. (How about that physical conditioning program?) We then began the tedious task of moving the trucks by placing the lids from the drone crates under the rear tires while pulling with the winch from the crane truck. Tired and relieved, we were finally ready for launch at 0200, 17 January 1991. What had taken us three hours to perform during training took us seven hours in the field. But we did it, and tension began to mount as 0300 rolled around. Soon, we'd see if our work had paid off.

Just prior to 0300, we heard an F-117 stealth fighter streak over our heads, low and fast, on its way to Baghdad. A few minutes later, Special Forces helicopters screamed over us, and the Iraqi forward positions about 10 miles in front of us began to explode on the horizon.

It was now time for us to do our part as the initial strike packages approached our area. I was crouched between the compressor vehicles, with the drones fired up and running on both sides of me. I carefully attached the cable to the 28VDC battery that would ignite the JATO bottles and send our drones on their way. As I watched the countdown on my stopwatch, I wondered what it would be like to launch one of these things. Finally, the seconds ticked down, and I threw the switches. My whole world turned bright yellow, and a huge explosion rocketed the first drone into the air. Quickly recovering from the initial jolt of seeing the drone go, I rippled off the remaining birds according to the timing plan.

We'd done it! The first package was on its way, and I could hear the flight cheering and screaming in the background. What a moment! There were several hours before the next package was due to go, so we had time to tune in the BBC on the shortwave radio. It was a thrill to stand there in the desert and listen to the broadcasters describe the air strike as it happened outside the windows of their hotel in Baghdad. It was time to rotate the happy and exhausted men into a well-deserved rest cycle while maintaining perimeter security.

We remained in the field for two more days, performing several follow-on missions. We were fortunate that the air threat was practically nonexistent; we didn't have to move at all. As for mission success, according to *Aviation Week & Space Technology,* "Electronics intelligence data showed a dramatic decrease in Iraqi electronic activity within the first 72 hours of the war. Finally, the Iraqis resorted to simply shooting their missiles without turning on radar when allied aircraft were in the area." We returned to base without incident after shooting over 20 drones into Iraq.

You're in the Army Now?

by

Capt Donald A. Koehler

When I joined the Air Force in 1986, we made a few agreements. In exchange for good pay, excellent benefits, and a great way of life, I was reasonably expected to go to war if my country required it . . . in an airplane. They spent over a million dollars to make me the best C-130 navigator ever. So how did I end up fighting Desert Storm with the Army?

I volunteered! But it was never supposed to happen this way. I've always enjoyed running around with the Army on training exercises, and a colonel (whom I promised not to incriminate) told me I could go to Tactical Airlift Liaison Officer's School and do it part-time. How was I supposed to know Iraq would invade Kuwait, and the US would take offense? The next thing I knew, I was part of the "Line in the Sand." And I mean there was sand as far as the eye could see. I found myself in a little known and less understood career field, where I was responsible for coordinating and controlling any airlift my Army unit might need. I was assigned to a tank regiment. Now these guys understood "flying tanks" (helicopters) pretty well, but "flying trucks" (C-130s) were new to them. I had my work cut out for me.

On 17 January 1991, I joined the 2d Armored Cavalry Regiment (2 ACR) in northern Saudi Arabia. Although these fine people wore Army uniforms and drove M-1A1 tanks, they were CAVALRY soldiers, one generation removed from George Armstrong Custer, and definitely just as crazy. Their mission in Europe was to draw Warsaw Pact forces out of column formation and into battle formation. This sounds great, but they weren't expected to survive the encounter. The "Cav" was proud of this. I was worried. Our mission in Iraq was to range ahead of the main line of armored forces (gulp!), reconnoiter Republican Guard positions by fire (GULP!), and then bypass pockets of resistance as we advanced, leaving them in our rear areas for the armored divisions to deal with (Mommy!)!! This is precisely what happened, with a few minor alterations to the plan.

Anyone who was there can tell you that Desert Storm occurred during the wettest winter on record. The rain kept the dust down— and a desert thunderstorm shouldn't be missed! But the tractor-trailers the Army uses to haul ammunition and fuel sunk in the mud. Did this slow down the 2d Cavalry? Did Custer let a little thing like being outnumbered five-to-one slow him down?

By day two of the ground war, the 2d ACR was short of everything, especially tank and artillery ammunition. And of course, at this precise moment, we slammed into the Tawakalna division of the Republican Guard. The mayhem was incredible. I spent most of that night screaming into a radio to anyone who would listen that we needed airlift resupply at first light. (A word about Army tactical communications. They use microwave telephones that work very well when you are in range. We weren't in range.) The Air Force, in its wisdom, had provided me with a satellite radio. Once I convinced everyone else to clear the net, things went along fine.

I didn't get my airlift at first light, but I got it. The tank drivers laughed as I chased the one-ton bundles of high explosives across the desert. The wind blew 32 bundles straight away from me at 25 mph. The only way to stop them was to drive in front of them and collapse the parachutes.

Then they were mad at me for breaking the mirrors off of my HMMWV! That's gratitude for you. Actually, the cavalry repaid the favor the same day. My column managed to drive right through our front lines and into a waiting platoon of T-72 tanks. Since I didn't have an Army radio in my vehicle, my first notion that something was amiss was when my column leader passed me, going the other way! About the time I Bat-turned (and the Iraqis found our range), I saw the most beautiful sight mortal man could ever behold: six Cobra gunships firing TOW missiles right over our heads. The Iraqis died, we lived, and Army aviators are now demigods in my eyes.

M-1A1 Tank Crossing the Saudi-Iraqi Border

Fun in the Sand

Movin' On

Dead T-72 Tank in Iraq

Former Mortar Carrier

The next morning, our role in the war ended. The armored divisions finally caught up and passed us on their way to finish off the Republican Guard. The next thing I know, we're sitting in Kuwait watching oil fires. Awesome! Second Cav inherited Ali Salam Military Airfield, 10 miles west of Kuwait City. It was usable, but the Iraqis left stripped vehicles on the runways and the USAF left me enough antipersonnel mines to go into business for myself. With a lot of help from some engineers, we cleared the field just in time to land one C-130 before the Cav got orders back to Iraq. We pulled back about 80 miles due west, where I found the airdrop bundles we had lost earlier.

The last part of my adventure with 2d ACR took me to the Euphrates River and the ancient city of Ur. By now, the Air Force people had pooled themselves together for traveling and camping purposes. Collectively, we had a generator, a VCR, a 25-inch Sony TV, and lawn chairs. (Doesn't everybody go to war properly

107

Gee, Mom, Can I Keep It?

Captured T-72 in Iraq

Dead T-55s in Kuwait

equipped?) We were told to meet the Cav at point "X," and our global positioning system (GPS) had a firm lock on the target.

But the GPS is only as smart as the fool who's using it. The problem was the road veered off 90 degrees from where the GPS said we needed to go. So we followed the autopilot (GPS) straight across Iraqi farmland. It was night, the rain was pouring down, and the dirt bridges over the irrigation ditches were not as wide as the HMMWV tires. But we were good Boy Scouts—we were prepared. We stopped in a small field, posted guards, and hit the sack!

Iraq was fighting the Shiites by this time. Close inspection of area maps later revealed that we had been smack in the middle of "Indian country." I awoke to the sound of Iraqi heavy machine-gun fire. There were 14 of us. We had one M-16, two or three AK-47s, and fourteen 9-mm pistols. Fighting was out of the question, and we couldn't run away. In the end, we were saved by geography. The field we were in had a deep ditch all around it. The Shiites backed up to it and went around. The Iraqis advanced up to it and went around. It was dark, they didn't see us. At first light, we hightailed back to the road, found some tank tracks and linked up with our forces. Soon afterwards, I rotated back to a rear area and then back to a grateful nation.

I want to end this story with some very important lessons learned. No one expected to fight this kind of war and, as a result, we had to make up a lot of tactics as we went along. Armored forces normally use little airlift and less airdrop. They move tonnages that are incomprehensible to airlifters. In a fast-paced offensive war, the logistical train can derail too easily. Airdropping just a little ammunition at the right place and time turned the battle at a crucial point and saved American lives. The Air Force needs to be smarter about what it can do for the Army in a tight spot. We all need to understand why we exist, and whom we are here to support. We got a great reputation out of Desert Storm. Let's not forget that brave men and women hung it out in the tanks, trucks, helicopters, and HMMWVs. I'll close with the motto of the 2d Armored Cavalry Regiment: *Toujours Pret!* That translates, "Always Ready!" They were. They are. I'm proud I was with them.

US Army Hospitality

War: My Reality

by

Capt Larry Bostrom

War! The word means different things to different people, depending on their life experience. My involvement in Operation Desert Shield/Desert Storm showed me, firsthand, the realities of war. Initially, the prospect of war flooded me with the mixed emotions of excitement, fear, and determination. I had only seen war through the eyes of others. Finally, I would have the opportunity to use the knowledge and skills I had developed in years of training as a pilot in the RF-4C tactical reconnaissance aircraft.

Sensationalism turned to realism after my first few weeks in Saudi Arabia. I realized no exercises or training programs can prepare you for all aspects of war. And General Schwarzkopf's book (*In the Eye of the Storm*) affirms that: "The Gulf operation was led by men who were lieutenants, captains, majors and lieutenant colonels in Vietnam. From up close they had all seen jaws shot off, limbs amputated, young lives extinguished. This experience changed them."

In August 1990, when Operation Desert Shield began, there were only two active duty RF-4 squadrons stateside: the 91st Tactical Reconnaissance Squadron (TRS) "Demon Chasers" (my squadron), and the 12th TRS "Blackbirds." Rumor said that one of the two squadrons would deploy to the desert. I figured I had a 50/50 shot at going, but my squadron lost the toss. The good news was that the 12th TRS needed a liaison officer at Central Air Forces (CENTAF) headquarters in Riyadh, Saudi Arabia. I quickly volunteered. I had to be involved some way.

I arrived in Riyadh just days before the war began, and I quickly tried to learn my new job. I was assigned to the 597th Tactical Air Control Center, in the plans shop. My job was to build the reconnaissance portion of the daily air tasking order (ATO). The ATO is a "play book" of the war, describing everyone's mission and the coordination needed to carry out the day's war plan. On the surface, the task seemed quite simple. Like a puzzle, each person was responsible for one piece. However, when bullets start flying, not all the pieces always fit. As an aircraft commander, I had only been responsible for myself and one other crew member. The stakes were higher now—my actions affected a squadron of aircraft and crew. Any mistakes I made could be paid for with someone's life.

A typical day in the office started around 0600. During the night, requests for reconnaissance photos came in and were prioritized. It was then up to me to match these requests with the day's available sorties. There were sometimes 75 or more targets to be placed in the ATO. For each target, exact coordinates and photo requirements were translated into a long series of alphanumeric codes. After I turned in the final draft of the ATO, I would check the photo results from the previous day. I ensured that requests were filled properly and that the information was going to the people who needed it. On days when the weather was bad, I made last-minute changes. We scrambled to ensure the coordination was perfect and that crews were protected as much as possible. My friends were flying these missions; if I couldn't help them in the air, I would do whatever I could from the ground.

As the days rolled on, I found myself growing numb to the war outside my office. Scud missile attacks, although common, were ineffective. I dismissed them as a threat to me. The Iraqis never tried to send a strike force out to bomb us, and I was confident we could easily defeat it if they tried. But as I became complacent, something happened to bring me back to reality. One day a soldier accidently discharged his M-16 in the compound outside CENTAF headquarters, and the word spread through the building quickly. First we heard, "there was gunfire in the compound." Then, "gunfire in the building." Finally someone shouted, "gunfire in the hallway!" and we all dove under our desks for cover. We were relieved to find it was only an accident, but I stopped and thought about the war outside.

A few days later, a courier delivered battle damage assessment (BDA) photos from the previous day's missions. Included were the usual bridges, airfields, bunkers, and command posts, but I looked at them a bit differently. I realized that these were not just objects being destroyed; people's lives were being destroyed also. On many occasions, I had to coordinate with the people in the targeting cell, affectionately called the "Black Hole" because people went in but never came out. In the hole, I saw videotapes of actual weapons deliveries, and I watched bombs hit their targets. Seeing some of the realities of war, close-up, was sobering. I was beginning to change. Unfortunately, it would take more than photos and videos to drive the point home. The clincher came one night on my way home from work.

I was living in Eskan village, about 20 kilometers southeast of Riyadh. Buses ran 24 hours a day, taking us to and from our offices. The trip usually lasted 40 to 45 minutes, depending on the route we took. During the trip I usually read or caught up on much-needed sleep. After an 18-hour day, I boarded the bus ready to sleep my way home, knowing it would be only six short hours until I returned to work. On the way home, we were alerted by radio of an incoming Scud missile attack. My first feelings were, "Great! Another useless mask drill." The bus driver pulled to the side of the road under an overpass, and we waited. Suddenly the whole bus shook and the windows rattled. Nearly 15 minutes passed before we started back on our way. As the bus driver pulled out from under the overpass, my eyes focused on a huge fireball. A Scud missile had landed less than a mile away, just missing a residential neighborhood, just missing me. The war came to me that night.

My experience in the Gulf War has truly changed my life. I walked away with a new understanding of war itself, and now I place a greater value on human life. There are no winners in war—one side simply loses less than the other.

I am proud to have served in the Gulf War, and I believe it was necessary. Moreover, I am thankful that our leaders had a true understanding of all the aspects of war. Their decisions reflected the preciousness of life and the necessity for swift victory. We will not always be able to deter war; however, when next called upon, we will fight with the full understanding of the realities of war.

115

Dragon City, Saudi Arabia, 9 January–9 March 1991

by

Capt Michael Joy

When the air campaign began, I was assigned to XVIII Airborne Corps as a liaison between Corps G2 and the national intelligence community. The Defense Intelligence Agency (DIA) sent me over on 9 January. My job was to monitor a radio network that provided voice and data reports from Washington to the units in and around Saudi Arabia from 0700–2100. Our radio network, the national military intelligence support team (NMIST) network, carried primarily strategic intelligence reports. Tactical intelligence and operational information were forbidden on the net except for those who were under attack.

For the first two hours of the air campaign, the radio emitted a steady hiss, broken by an occasional radio check from one of the 11 teams on the network. If it wasn't for CNN, we'd have wondered whether or not we were at war.

Over the next few days, radio traffic increased as we received battle damage assessments, downed-pilot reports, daily summaries of targets, and twice-daily battlefield assessments.

I had received half-a-dozen immunizations and handfuls of pills to ward off all the ills of the desert and protect me against a variety of chemical weapons. On the eve of the air war, we began taking a new pill every six hours to facilitate a nerve agent antidote injector that we carried with our gas masks. The main side effect I experienced was dehydration. I drank over a quart of water an hour to combat the thirst and the desert crud in the back of my throat.

What goes in must come out, and about 0200 on 18 January my distended bladder woke me and demanded I trek 100 yards to the latrine. When I got up and approached the tent flap, I heard a loud

117

explosion outside. The ground shook and the canvas rippled with the concussion. I knew my M-16 was no match for the boom I heard, but my bladder beckoned me on, and I carefully emerged from the tent. Centered in the clear sky about one mile east of us was a huge smoky octopus. Thousands of tentacle-like smoke trails emerged from a central blast, each making their way toward the ground. Whatever had just occurred looked like it was over, so I continued on my way. In the morning, I found that this was the first Scud targeted at Dhahran. A Patriot battery to the northeast took it out. Go Army!

After completing my indoctrination around Dragon City (Corps headquarters in Dhahran) I switched to the 1900–0700 shift. Team Chief Capt Tim Bloecl, USA, split the team into one officer and two enlisted per shift in preparation for split team operations as the Corps moved 400 miles to the northwest. The move was weeks away, but we wanted to identify any shortfalls in our equipment and procedures before it came.

Although the air attacks kept Iraq's Scud launchers under cover during the day, nighttime was a different story. Scud launch reports interrupted the radio hiss, giving the number of missiles, launch time, location, and azimuth. The reports to our radio network lagged actual launch by four minutes. Operation nets for the Patriots or ground attack squadrons were more time-sensitive than ours since we were not a critical node.

The chemical threat received a lot of airtime in message traffic and on CNN. When a missile headed my way, my pulse rate rose. The entire unit donned masks and chemical suits in anticipation of the worst. I wondered about equipment quality.

Some Scuds were intercepted in the sky, others were deemed nonthreatening and allowed to dig holes in the desert around us. After each one, we cheered the Patriots and waited for the "all clear" before we removed our masks. A dozen Scuds targeted our area before our unit moved in February.

One particular night, the message traffic indicated an elevation to chemical weapons. So many Scuds and so many earlier threats of chemical usage were unfounded, I almost became complacent. There was something about this warning though—multiple launches from multiple locations! Targets: Riyadh and Dhahran.

The four minutes between the radio report and expected impact was interminable. My heart pounded in my ears, and I could see the obvious tension on 60 other faces through the bug eyes of their gas masks. The explosion blew the double doors inward on their hinges. Sand and paper rode the rush of air into the SCIF. Anxiety turned to fear as we felt the blast of air against our protective gear; but that fear was quickly pushed aside and replaced with action. Everyone monitored their chemical indicator tape for a reaction, checked others for indication of contamination, and ensured masks and suits were leak-free. We radioed to hear if Riyadh was OK. Thirty minutes later, we heard the all clear. No chemicals! The blast had tipped over my antenna, but otherwise Dragon City was undamaged. Close call!

We moved the headquarters in two 40-vehicle convoys. One-half went up in late January, and the remainder on 3 February. I was supposed to be part of the second convoy when a C-130 became available to move 24 people, equipment, and a vehicle to our new location at Rafhã airport.

During this move, my admiration for the Army grew. I watched while my tentmates packed their rucksacks. I tried to ask intelligent questions before attempting this feat myself. I packed a helmet bag with a survival kit during a previous assignment, and I geared up to hike the Appalachian Trail; but my Air Force training fell a bit short when tents, convoys, and rucksacks entered the conversation. After I endured some well-earned ribbing, the warrant officers helped me through.

Over a pork patty MRE at the airport, I heard an age-old substitute for the MAC acronym—Maybe Aircraft Come. As the only blue suiter, I defended my transportation brethren. After another hour, I understood the genesis of this substitute.

When the aircraft came, we gathered our gear and piled it in the rear of the plane. We strapped ourselves into the four rows of facing web seats, knees and feet searching for neutral territory across the aisle for the 90-minute flight. I was as comfortable as my six-foot, five-inch frame allowed, but my Army buddies looked uncomfortable

119

without the parachutes they usually wore on these flights. Their anxiety disappeared as we approached the runway. As the aircraft stopped with the ramp open, we deplaned equipment, vehicle, and everything else in three minutes.

The base at Rafhā had been converted from a Saudi military/civilian airport. The main terminal housed the headquarters and most of the operations work. NMIST was next door in a concrete maintenance facility with the targeteers, special operations, and a host of downlinks from Army field units. We had time before the ground campaign commenced to firm up the Corps plan of action. We coordinated with the signals and imagery folks to provide local operations and tactical data back to CENTCOM and Washington, and requested targeting and other information in return. Special operations requested additional information to fine-tune their plans. Information from Iraqi prisoners was of high interest—chemical artillery shell markings and locations, biographical data, and the general morale and status of enemy forces topped the list of queries.

As G-day approached, our area received more attention. More tactical reconnaissance was available and more air strikes were made (we could see the blue-white flashes in the night sky from B-52 strikes). Teams triangulated a final fix on enemy radar and radio sites. The war had finally come for the Army. To a person, everyone in the Corps had hoped that the war would be averted, but now that it had started, the Corps wanted to be a part of finishing the job.

The ground war moved lightning-fast from our perspective. Every time I came on shift it was a new war. Hundreds of square miles of Iraqi territory were under Corps control. Reams of information poured in, all good! Intelligence had done its job. Every target was right where we said it was, and the Army and Air Force methodically removed them from the threat list. In fact, the Corps ate up ground so fast that requests for intelligence during the latter stages of this phase were often canceled because the Army captured the target before intelligence assets could address them.

The tactical system that impressed me most was J-STARS. I visited the ground link stationed with us twice per shift. I watched as our forces raced through Iraqi territory and as Iraqi forces headed to Basra for the only remaining highway route to Baghdad. J-STARS data was used very effectively to vector coalition aircraft toward enemy troop movements. When columns of Iraqi armor moved from their entrenchments, A-10s swarmed within minutes. I could only wonder how much longer the war would have lasted without J-STARS capability.

One week after the ground war halted, NMIST loaded up on a French C-160 bound for Riyadh. After a one-hour layover, a C-5 took us to Dover AFB, Delaware, via Torrejon AB, Spain. The Army took good care of me; I hoped the Air Force would bring them home quickly. As I climbed aboard the C-5, I altered the MAC acronym once more—My Aircraft Come. God bless my friends in the Army. God bless America!

NAVSTAR GPS Operations

by

Capt Michael P. Scardera

A Tour through NAVSTAR GPS Space Operations

Twenty people walk into a dark room in June 1990. Two small satellite models spin around a rotating 18-inch globe, their little solar panels track the "artificial sun" spotlight.

"Welcome to the NAVSTAR global positioning system (GPS) master control station (MCS) operated by the 2d Satellite Control Squadron. I'm Capt Mike Scardera, a navigation analyst here in the MCS. The GPS provides accurate navigation services to military and civilian users around the world any time of day, every day of the year. Each satellite transmits its positions at a given time, so anyone equipped with a GPS receiver can calculate a range to any satellite visible overhead. Four ranges from four different satellites mathematically provide the receiver's latitude, longitude, altitude, and time error in a process similar to triangulation. Military users can determine their position to within 10 meters while civilian users, without proper code decryption equipment, receive about 100 meters of navigation accuracy."

"The NAVSTAR system includes 24 operational Block II satellites to ensure that four satellites are overhead anywhere on the Earth. Since February 1989, we've launched seven Block II satellites, the highest launch rate since the 1960s. These new spacecraft join the six aging research and development Block I satellites launched to prove the GPS concept. Twenty-four Block II satellites should be working in 1993."

Pointing towards the dynamic GPS model, the briefer continues: "Each satellite's solar panels constantly track the Sun for power to operate the spacecraft systems. Batteries power the satellite when it passes through the Earth's shadow. The satellite's control systems produce telemetry which help us track its health and status. Complex computers and atomic clocks produce navigation information. Each satellite has four spinning reaction wheels, one of which is a reserve spare. Three spinning wheels are required to keep the radio antenna pointed towards Earth."

The tour continued at the glassed-off master control station's "fishbowl." "Every satellite must be in good working order, accurately transmitting its position and time for GPS navigation to work properly. The NAVSTAR GPS master control station, located here at Falcon AFB, Colorado, is responsible for the health and maintenance of GPS spacecraft and their navigation systems. Five monitor stations located around the world receive the same radio transmissions that GPS users receive. These stations transfer the information to the MCS, where the navigation data is processed through complicated mathematical models in order to accurately predict the satellite's future positions. Four large ground antennas, also located around the world, upload the improved predictions and update the information broadcast by the satellites. Notice also that everyone in the fishbowl is a blue suiter. We are proud to be one of the few satellite systems that is entirely Air Force-operated."

Following the tour, a woman asked, "Since you don't have all 24 satellites in orbit yet, how much can people use GPS now?"

"Currently there are seven operational Block II satellites: NAVSTARs 13, 14, 16, 17, 18, 19, and 20. There are also six old research and development satellites still in orbit, NAVSTARs 3, 6, 8, 9, 10, and 11. These 13 GPS spacecraft currently provide about 12 hours of three-dimensional coverage and 20 hours of two-dimensional coverage to any location around the world."

A pilot then asked a fairly common question, "How does your job change when there's a war?"

"Our mission in war is the same as in peace. In essence, space operators are at war every day."

NAVSTAR Master Control Station, Falcon AFB, Colorado

Maximizing GPS Middle East Coverage

Working as a GPS navigation analyst was fun and exciting, but the hours were especially long from February 1989 to July 1990 because we launched seven new Block II satellites. The Air Force launched its eighth Block II GPS satellite, NAVSTAR 21, on 2 August, the same day Iraqi forces invaded Kuwait. As the United States began deploying troops to Saudi Arabia, there was tremendous pressure to put the newest NAVSTAR on-line as soon as possible.

In the year prior to Desert Shield, I learned how to shorten the time for navigation payload activation. When the first operational NAVSTAR was launched, we took 30 days to activate the navigation payload. I learned many lessons about choosing the best computer parameters and automating procedures over the subsequent launches. By the time Iraq invaded Kuwait, the navigation payload initialization had been reduced to 14 days. The MCS started to reposition GPS

125

satellites in the spring of 1990 to optimize worldwide navigation coverage. Each satellite fires small thrusters to change its orbit. Thruster firing disturbs the models, which predict the satellite's orbital position. Later, MCS corrects the orbit models to resume navigation service. After drifting to their new positions, the thrusters fire again to stop the satellites. Prior to 1990, a thruster firing took a satellite off the air for three or four days while the MCS recovered the orbit models. By analyzing the data from the repositioning effort's start in 1990, consulting with other engineers, and performing controlled tests, I was able to improve MCS technical capabilities, improve maneuver models, refine procedures, and reduce outage time to about 10 hours. The improved navigation recovery was available for the end of the NAVSTAR repositioning effort in the fall of 1990, coincident with Desert Shield. Simultaneously, I discovered an attribute in the system software which could consistently reduce the outage time to four hours, but I couldn't implement this simple change because further maneuver testing was prohibited at the start of Desert Shield.

I couldn't convince my superiors that the benefits of the new method were worth the risks until NAVSTAR 21's last scheduled positioning maneuver. Because we couldn't set the satellite healthy (in good condition) on the planned day, my superiors allowed me to use the new technique to try to meet the deadline. By reprocessing 12 hours of data, using the new technique, we made the satellite available without delay.

These lessons helped us to save time with other satellite maintenance as well. I applied some of the navigation payload initialization lessons to satellite navigation system adjustments and atomic clock adjustments. Lt Cordell Fox automated many procedures, and we shortened payload maintenance outage time from a full day to four or five hours. Consequently, the nine separate satellite maneuvers required for constellation optimization and numerous maintenance activities did not reduce GPS availability over the Persian Gulf.

NAVSTAR 15, launched on 1 October 1990, reached its final orbit in 9 days. When Lt Col William Shelton, the new 2d Satellite Control Squadron commander, asked for the fastest possible navigation payload initialization, my immediate supervisor, Capt Dave Koster, promised to set the satellite in six days. I calmly approached Dave and said, "Dave, we need to talk."

Dave sighed, "What do you want?"

"Kyle just said that you told Colonel Shelton we'd have NAVSTAR 15 set healthy in six days!"

Sensing my mood, he diplomatically replied, "I didn't think there'd be a problem since we can apply all the stuff you've learned on satellite maneuvers and clock maintenance."

"Yeah, but you didn't even ask me! I'm your most experienced analyst. Payload initialization isn't that straightforward. With satellite maneuvers, the clock stays stable; and with clock maintenance, the orbit is stable. When a new payload is initialized, both the orbit and clock are highly uncertain and the system models have a hard time sorting out the errors between the two."

Dave hit below the belt with his next statement. "Look, there are a lot of people out in the Persian Gulf depending on us. Are you saying you can't do your best for them?"

"Look, Dave, you know more than anyone else I'll do my best and I will put my best efforts into reducing the initialization period from 14 days to six, but I still think it's foolish to guarantee six days to the commander. It's like the weatherman saying it'll be sunny next Monday. His forecast techniques may allow him to say so with confidence, but there's no way he could guarantee it."

Dave replied, "I'm not going to change what I've already told Colonel Shelton, so we'll have to try our best. If we don't make it in six days we'll explain why then."

I was satisfied with that final response. Although I would often disagree with many of Dave Koster's methods, I couldn't argue anymore with his leadership on this issue.

I pushed the system limits to make this satellite available by 16 October, only six days. Pushing limits is very risky because less accurate GPS signals are likely before the satellite's navigation systems stabilize. I worked around the clock, monitoring and massaging NAVSTAR 15's computer models. I tried some of the new techniques, but with the uncertainties and cross errors of initialization, some of those techniques may have hurt as much as helped.

On day six, NAVSTAR 15's navigation performance was barely meeting specifications. It wasn't even close to the normally expected GPS performance. But Colonel Shelton considered the added GPS availability to Desert Shield troops a higher priority than perfect accuracy. So, tender loving care was the watchword, and NAVSTAR 15's navigation performance stabilized about a week and a half later. The performance was not the best during this time, but navigation was well within system specifications. Colonel Shelton had set a precedent.

Keeping Broken Satellites Working

The Air Force launched the first new generation Block IIA NAVSTAR spacecraft, NAVSTAR 23, on 23 November 1990. On 29 November 1990 the United Nations passed Resolution 678, authorizing military force to evict Iraq from Kuwait after 15 January 1991. US Space Command accelerated the GPS launch schedule to provide full 24-satellite navigation capability as soon as possible. Those plans came to an abrupt halt when the automatic system which controlled NAVSTAR 23's solar panels failed. We could not launch any additional GPS satellites until the Air Force had diagnosed and fixed the problem. In the meantime, GPS operations crews manually positioned NAVSTAR 23's solar panels, an unusual and critical task that had to be repeated up to four times each 12-hour orbit to ensure that power was supplied and the satellite maintained a proper position.

Despite the solar panel problem, NAVSTAR 23 was producing normal navigation data within a week. On 21 December, Capt Tom Carrington noticed NAVSTAR 23 was producing range errors just large enough to prevent the system from updating the navigation models. I came down from my office, signed on at an empty control console, and determined that NAVSTAR 23's clock had failed. There was some debate about the source of the problem, but we eventually switched the atomic clocks to redundant units. They stabilized one week before the 15 January 1991 ultimatum.

We faced other problems as well. NAVSTAR 3's solar panels had slowly deteriorated and one of its three batteries had failed since it was launched (in 1978), so it couldn't generate enough power for eclipse season operations. In the summer 1990 eclipse season, the MCS turned off NAVSTAR 3's navigation payload when the satellite batteries could no longer support a pass through the earth's shadow. NAVSTAR 3 would be over the Middle East and in the earth's shadow during the January 1991 eclipse season, so we turned off the payload when NAVSTAR 3 was over the South Atlantic to give the solar panels enough time to fully recharge the two batteries before eclipse, thus protecting users in the Middle East. By the end of December 1990, full 24-hour two-dimensional coverage was available to the Desert Shield coalition forces. Three-dimensional coverage increased from 12 to 21 hours each day.

NAVSTAR in the Field

Resurrecting a Dead Satellite

On 10 December 1991, the same day we originally set NAVSTAR 23 healthy, NAVSTAR 6 suffered a catastrophic failure. Each NAVSTAR needs three of its four reaction wheels to keep its radio transmission antennas pointed continuously towards earth. NAVSTAR 6 lost one reaction wheel in 1987, and thrusters began maintaining its orientation when it lost a second wheel on 10 December. NAVSTAR 6 was low on fuel because it was 10 years old, and we had used much of its fuel to recover from previous failures. If we lost NAVSTAR 6, we would lose two hours of three-dimensional coverage. And because we might also lose NAVSTAR 3, 23, or another NAVSTAR satellite in addition to NAVSTAR 6, the situation was desperate.

Capt Gary Freeland, the 2d Satellite Control Squadron's lead satellite systems engineer, came up with a radical idea. On 17 December Gary asked in a conspiratorial whisper, "Mike, can I ask you a question?"

"Sure Gary, what is it?" He continued in a low tone, "Is there any way your wizardry can model NAVSTAR 6 with thrusters firing every 6 hours?"

Gary often joked that operating the GPS navigation system was akin to witchcraft. He was right, in that GPS navigation operations are as much art as straightforward engineering. I shook my head, "No, I don't think so. We might be able to maintain about 100-meter accuracy with it, but I really think the uncertainties building up just continue to get worse. Besides, how bad is the fuel situation?"

"Right now we're projecting the satellite will be out of fuel by January sixth." He paused for a second. "If I told you I could successfully spin-stabilize the satellite and point it towards Kuwait, can you do your hocus pocus and get any useful information out of it?"

I had to ponder a minute. He proposed spinning the satellite to maintain attitude control. A spinning satellite doesn't need reaction wheels or thrusters, but the transmission antennas would sweep past the earth only once per orbit. Spinning the satellite would initially increase orbit uncertainty, and the atomic clock might undergo a slight change in behavior due to different operating temperatures.

Once spun up, the satellite would be stable but it would receive only a fraction of the data normally needed for good navigation predictions. Despite the concerns, I optimistically answered, "Well, I think we should be able to get at least 100-meters accuracy consistently, which is better than nothing. By pulling some tricks, I think we could do better, but I really couldn't tell you without trying it."

We discussed the idea with others in the squadron and eventually sent it up the chain of command. Despite the unknowns in spin-stabilized GPS navigation, Lieutenant General Moorman, commander of Air Force Space Command, approved the attempt to resurrect NAVSTAR 6.

Gary Freeland organized a meeting on 20 December with design engineers from Rockwell to discuss the configuration. Gary presented the situation and his proposal for NAVSTAR 6. Then he opened the floor for discussion.

The spacecraft engineers were very pessimistic. One engineer said, matter-of-factly, "When the antennas are pointed toward the Sun they may delaminate. We don't know how the antennas will work if they come apart." Another added, "Even worse than that, the batteries might explode with the Sun on them a half-revolution later in the orbit." A third engineer said, "Even if the batteries don't explode or the antennas don't delaminate, my analysis shows we can only get about a half-hour of navigation. Can you do anything with that?"

I answered the last question quickly, "No, a half-hour wouldn't be enough, but my calculations show at least an hour and a half when navigation signals could be observed, and we may get up to two hours depending on whether or not we can see any transmission side lobes."

I soon left the meeting, but I couldn't believe the gloom and doom presented by the Rockwell engineers. That evening, I rechecked my figures on the signal availability and performed some back-of-the-envelope calculations on the temperature variations to be sure.

The next day, I told Gary my original calculations on visibility checked out. The spinning satellite should have a slightly higher than normal temperature throughout the orbit. Spinning the satellite actually reduced temperature extremes during its orbit.

Gary said he had performed similar calculations with the same results. He dubbed spin stabilization the "rotisserie" mode of operation, and we quickly developed many novel procedures and techniques. I set up several different system data base files to handle different situations. I also drew out a detailed plan of action for NAVSTAR 6's spin-stabilized navigation payload initialization. I finished preparing the computer data bases and written plans after NAVSTAR 23's clock problems had been diagnosed.

GPS operations crews fired NAVSTAR 6's thrusters on 27 December 1990, spinning the satellite up to 2.5 rotations per minute with satellite radio transmission antennas pointed toward Kuwait City. The satellite engineers carefully monitored the power and thermal situation for 24 hours. Gary and his engineers had done their job. Now the work turned to the navigation analysts.

Captain Koster determined that the radio signals swept past the Persian Gulf for 100 minutes. The transmission side lobes didn't add any time. Between visibility windows, crew operators turned off the radio transmitters to conserve power. The navigation analysts started the initialization procedures I had drawn up. After one day, range errors from NAVSTAR 6 were 300 meters; not bad! I worked long hours with rare programs to try to improve navigation accuracy. Late one night, Capt Chris Langone, another navigation analyst, asked why I was expending so much effort on this worthless satellite. I answered, "With so many troops about to go to war, the least I can do is to get something useful out of this satellite if it's at all possible."

I asked the GPS test personnel at the US Army's Yuma Proving Ground to track NAVSTAR 6 over the weekend. I created and installed some data base files that adjusted the MCS models, compensating for the uncertainties in estimating both the satellite's orbit and atomic clock time. On Saturday, 5 January 1991, NAVSTAR 6 produced range errors as low as 10 meters! Twelve hours later, over Diego Garcia, navigation range errors grew to 200 meters. That would not do!

I created and installed different files on Sunday. They produced 40-meter accuracy over Yuma and 20-meters over Diego Garcia. This was better, but not good enough. I created and installed one final series of data base files for Monday, then I headed off to Washington DC for meetings. While I was in Washington, Dave Koster turned off an automatic range-error checking routine. This combination was perfect, and range errors were consistently 10–20 meters. Capt Chris Langone rallied several GPS manufacturers to monitor navigation performance with NAVSTAR 6. According to all the manufacturers he contacted, NAVSTAR 6 was usable. On 16 January 1991, US Space Command approved making NAVSTAR 6 data available to the users.

On 18 January 1991 the Joint Chiefs of Staff, at the urging of personnel in the GPS Joint Program Office, ordered NAVSTAR 6 off the air. Apparently, they didn't understand the need for NAVSTAR 6, the performance stability, or the independent checks we made.

Everyone in the 2d Satellite Control Squadron was upset. Colonel Shelton quickly arranged to brief the chain of command. Colonel Shelton, Major Fauver (user interface chief), Dr John Berg (Aerospace Corporation analyst), and I prepared a presentation explaining the contribution, capabilities, performance, and risks associated with operating NAVSTAR 6. Colonel Shelton briefed Col Barry Springer, acting commander of the 2d Space Wing. Dr Berg and I came along to answer technical questions. The next morning, Colonel Springer, Colonel Shelton, and I went to brief Brigadier General Gray, Air Force Space Command's director of operations at Peterson AFB, Colorado. Colonel Springer convinced General Gray, who sent us across the street to US Space Command headquarters.

After briefing the acting US Space Command director of operations (Colonel Cleveland), we entered CINCSPACE's office. General Kutyna was eating breakfast from a tray and watching Cable News Network. His manner was imperious. After exchanging platitudes with Colonel Springer, he asked, "What brings you downtown?"

Colonel Springer responded, "We have a satellite which was ordered off the air by the offices of the Joint Chiefs. The satellite had an attitude control problem and the folks in the squadron

NAVSTAR in Space—GPS Block II Satellites

worked hard to recover a residual capability. The satellite performs worse than normal."

"That's the problem. Our folks out there need the best service we can provide," interrupted the general.

"Yes, but this satellite meets GPS specifications and it provides three-dimensional coverage when there otherwise wouldn't be any." Colonel Springer had General Kutyna's attention. By the end of the meeting, General Kutyna was satisfied. As we left the office, he said, "I'll see what I can do."

US Space Command returned NAVSTAR 6 to limited service on 2 February 1991. It remained healthy until 5 March, providing additional support for the air campaign and the 100-hour ground battle. After the hostilities ended, we permanently shut down the satellite's navigation payload. On 24 April 1991, the remaining onboard propellant was exhausted. The satellite was placed in its most benign condition and permanently shut down.

Warm Fuzzies

While most space operators didn't endure the hardships of theater deployment or the rigors and dangers of combat, NAVSTAR GPS operations personnel worked long and hard hours to ensure that the Middle East theater received the best possible navigation service. Increasing the GPS navigation system's overall coverage, availability, and accuracy, despite numerous obstacles, were only a few of many accomplishments during Desert Shield. The soldiers, sailors, and airmen never realized all the effort behind the highly accurate and available navigation service they received. This one fact is our greatest tribute. Blue-suit space operations certainly proved their worth and showed the world how decisive space systems can be during the recent war.

One of the most interesting Desert Storm stories was reported by Brig Gen Creighton Abrams, US Army, on National Public Radio: "One of our divisions captured an enemy division commander, and practically the first question they asked him was, 'How come you guys didn't figure out we were going out to the west?' The answer they got was, 'We knew you wouldn't go out to the west. Get lost out there. That's why we don't go out there, even though its our home turf.'

So one of the interrogators showed him a little GPS device and said, 'Haven't you ever seen this?'

'No, what's that?'

'We call it GPS. Push these little buttons here, it will talk to satellites, tell you where you are.'

'How accurate is it?'

'Oh, it will get down to about five meters.'

'Are you kidding me?'

'No.'

'Your division commanders have this?'

'No, our platoon leaders have it. They all got it.'

'Oh, my.' "

The tremendous strides in GPS operations in general, and particularly the innovative NAVSTAR 6 operation, vindicate the idea of uniformed personnel operating military satellites. Desert Storm was truly the first space war.

A Captain's Perspective on the Gulf War

by

Capt Edward P. O'Connell

On 7 August 1990, I left Mayport Naval Base, Florida, on board the USS *Saratoga* aircraft carrier. It was the first leg of a historic journey to the Middle East. I was an adviser/observer on a "training opportunity" between CINCLANT and the Defense Intelligence Agency (DIA). My status quickly changed as one of the largest military operations in US history received its code name: Desert Shield. As I made my way to the gangplank and up to the quarterdeck that first afternoon, I passed a gaggle of CNN reporters and Navy enlisted men, all looking at me with the same quizzical-turned-to-knowing look: an Air Force officer?

I found my quarters and reported to the carrier intelligence center (CVIC) where I would be working. The next day, CVIC's intelligence chief integrated me into the flow of work. The battle group commander's chief of intelligence, or N-2, tasked him to develop a background paper on the Iraqi Air Force. In turn, he asked me to do the substantive analysis. Copies of my analysis were disseminated to critical staff throughout the ship in the form of a background point paper. The N-2 subsequently briefed this assessment to the battle group commander, who received it quite favorably.

A short time later, the chief of flag strike operations asked me to join his Iraqi mission-planning team. I was given the requisite clearances and quickly pulled into the budding effort. The Navy does not have targeting officers. Typically, squadron pilots do their own weaponeering/targeting. In fact, some senior officers onboard berated me good-naturedly for "being too damn specialized." But in this instance I was glad I was; they needed the help.

The USS *Saratoga*

I assisted F-14, F/A-18, and A-6 pilots to select desired-mean-points-of-impact (DMPI), offset aiming points (OAP), and weaponeer targets, as well as to draw radar predictions and determine accurate coordinates. One of the pilots I discussed F-16 radar predictions with was Lt Jeffrey Zhaun. Neither of us knew that in a few months his battered face would be on magazine covers all across the country. He was very helpful, as were most *Saratoga* pilots, giving me a "data dump" on Navy munitions such as standoff land attack missile (SLAM) and Tomahawk land attack missile (TLAM). More-over, they seemed surprised to hear an intelligence officer (one from DIA no less) speaking their language. On the other hand, I also advised the squadron intelligence officers on enemy order-of-battle considerations. These officers were very junior in grade, but they enjoyed an excellent rapport with their pilots and often worked nearly 20 hours a day.

Working in the CVIC provided a rare insight into US Navy wartime preparations. In addition, I roamed the ship during breaks and took in some interesting sights. I observed flight operations at close quarters from the flight deck, and I watched pilots "catch the three wire"—an amazing feat by any measure. On several moonlit nights I watched nighttime carrier "traps," with the air boss and his crew, up on the ninth deck.

Flight Operations in the Mediterranean

Under a change of orders, we steamed at full speed toward the east Mediterranean. When we reached the Strait of Gibraltar, the ship's captain invited all 3,000 personnel on board onto the flight deck to take in the spectacular view. The sun was setting behind us as we observed the Rock of Gibraltar off the port beam and the beautiful hills of Africa off the starboard. We passed a Soviet merchant ship, only 100 yards away, as a small ferry skittered across our bow. It was an experience I'll never forget.

I was struck by the difference in the practice of common customs and courtesies between the Air Force and the Navy. Early on, I was standing in a long line at the small snack bar on board, behind some tough looking "career" chiefs. I was approached by a fresh-faced

139

ensign who stopped and urged me to proceed to the head of the line. I chuckled, and chalked this up to an interservice joke. I quickly learned this wasn't a joke, and I began to eat more regularly.

I learned a great deal more during this period than I would have during a normal TRANSLANT training opportunity. I saw firsthand how tactical planners used many DIA mission-planning materials. Both the CVIC and strike operations staffs were dependent on DIA support, which they generally held in high regard. I mused to myself why I had never seen this type of support for USAF combat wings. Historically, the Navy had conducted contingency operations far more frequently than the Air Force. Their mission preparation manuals were better than I had ever seen in TAC. Enlisted intelligence specialists trained me on various unfamiliar automated mission-planning and intelligence-disseminating systems.

I returned to DIA in late August, and I reported my observations on intelligence support (to the *Saratoga*) to representatives from the chief of naval operations (CNO)/OP-05, in the Pentagon. I commented to one Navy representative, interested in starting a joint target officer's course, that squadron intelligence officers, pilots, and bombardier-navigators (BN) needed more extensive training in target development and analysis.

My supervisor, Col Joel Litman, the chief of DIA's targeting division, didn't waste any time putting me to work. He wanted me to work on a new targeting project that would collect imagery on Iraq. I took my own unique approach. I asked for an enlisted US Army intelligence analyst, a few field-grade USAF reserve officers, and an enlisted US Navy Reserve imagery analyst. Then I set to work. I told my small team we needed any open-source pictures of Iraq for use in mission planning. They scoured the Washington area from libraries to archive buildings, looking for relevant photos. We found many photos, which we indexed and sent to CENTCOM for target study and battle damage assessment (BDA) purposes. After the war, I spoke to a friend from the CENTAF Black Hole; he said he never saw them. However, I discovered recently that various targeting cells forward and Special Operations Command used them to build target intelligence packages (TIP).

Defense Intelligence Analysis Center, Washington, D.C.

My next project was even more important. I was to prepare special adaptive planning target materials (ADTM) for a Scud strategy that I helped outline at DIA. A US Navy reservist, a former A-6 BN, and I used all-source imagery, including LANDSAT, to design mission-planning materials. We tailored these products toward the aircraft we felt were the best candidates for the Scud search mission. Two of our top civilian analysts briefed the initial product design a few days later to Generals Schwarzkopf, Horner, and Glosson, and they were quite impressed with our effort to help in the attack against Scuds, a priority CENTCOM mission. Still, General Schwarzkopf told us, "It'll be like trying to find a needle in a haystack." In retrospect, it seems we had no real frame of reference for dealing with a problem like this. Some things, of course, we didn't think of until after the war. Actually, I discovered later (in my studies at the Defense Intelligence College) that operational and organizational problems encountered in the "Great Scud Hunt" were eerily reminiscent of those encountered in Operation Crossbow—the search for V-1 and V-2 missiles during World War II.

Soon I became the project officer for an interagency effort to produce hundreds of ADTMs. After disseminating the first batch to USAF, USA, and USN units in-theater, we received calls requesting more ADTMs. Together with my small layout team, I also began designing mission cards for J-STARS and Scud reconnaissance crews. DIA forwarded over 5,000 ADTMs to the theater, as war looked more and more likely. Sadly again, after the war, one of the "Scud-hunter" pilots aboard the USS *America* told me, "I would have killed to have gotten a single one of these products . . . I never saw one."

In October, a contact in DIA told me a project would soon be under way to exploit important enemy equipment. I suggested to Colonel Litman that we become the Washington-based point of contact for the project and assign three activated USN reserve officers as primary project officers. Soon Admiral McConnell, the JCS/J-2, sponsored the project. I responded to guidance from DIA's director of foreign intelligence, Major General Carr, to disseminate our findings to the theater. I stayed in Washington, churning out planning materials while I coordinated with our now field-deployed reservists on collection requirements.

As Desert Storm approached, I was hired by the Target Materiel Program Office as an action officer. One of our staff members went to establish a target materiel office to help get materiels and information flowing down to the wings and to the Black Hole. I soon coordinated requests from CENTCOM, EUCOM, and CENTAF to the Defense Mapping Agency Aerospace Center (DMAAC) for precise points for targeting. We had already worked extensively with DMAAC on the ADTM project, and we processed over 1,000 such requests for accurate precision guided munitions (PGM) points for a variety of aircraft. In addition, I performed detailed weaponeering analysis on Iraq's hardened aircraft shelters (HAS) which was used later by some combat wings forward during the "Shelter Campaign." I also continued to help line up the thousands of requests for information on target materiels and data base entries coming in from all over the world.

In early January, my boss told me I would be heading to Saudi Arabia in the next few days. I quickly packed my bags, and my adrenaline was pumping. Shortly before departing for Andrews AFB, my boss called me at home and told me I would not be deploying to the theater. "Everyone was overly anxious about being overrun by Washington" and the "powers that be" shot my visit down. I was quite disappointed, but I had plenty to do back at DIA in the coming weeks before the air war kicked off.

A few nights into the war, a strange thing happened. I was advising one of our analysts at the Defense Intelligence Analysis Center (DIAC) on a bomb-damage-assessment "call" when I heard a voice mumble from the nearby TV, "My name is Jeffrey Zhaun . . . I am a Lieutenant in the United States Navy." I ran to the TV and stared in disbelief at the sight of badly bruised Lieutenants Zhaun and Weitzel parading before Iraqi TV. Then, like others watching at DIA, I became angry. Only months before, I had met them on the USS *Saratoga* and both seemed like nice fellows. I certainly didn't think I needed any more inspiration to support my buddies in-theater, but I received an extra dose anyway. The *Saratoga* had been a hard-luck ship historically, and this news seemed to bear that out. After I left the ship, several *Saratoga* sailors drowned off the coast of Haifa, Israel, when the small ferry carrying them overturned.

From the outset, it was obvious to me that CENTAF and CENTCOM were not coordinating with each other or with the wings on a working level. Like others, at higher levels, I had a few contacts in-theater myself, which I used to help me "see" what was going on so that I could better focus the support I was working back at DIA. Additionally, I learned that critical mission-planning materials and targeting intelligence from our physical vulnerability branch were not getting to the Black Hole planners or the combat units. I began passing target recommendations from DIA analysts and my own weaponeering strategies to Checkmate planners working for Col John Warden in the Pentagon, who filtered them to the Black Hole. I participated in some discussions there on plans for the upcoming "Shelter Campaign."

At the same time, I was told to respond through official channels to DIA's requests for information (RFI) coming from CENTAF/ CENTCOM and Congress regarding weaponeering and structural analysis of potential Scuds or nuclear, biological, and chemical (NBC) targets. Much of my time was spent running between the National Photographic Interpretation Center (NPIC), DIAC, at Bolling AFB, and the Pentagon. My training and experience as a targeteer was paying off. Not only did I have a good idea of what the combat units needed, but I realized that by "running through the trenches in Washington" I could pull a large amount of useful information together. This is what targeteers typically do best.

At another point later in the war, the Relocatable Target Program Office (RTPO) in the Pentagon asked me to develop a detailed weaponeering and tactics strategy to neutralize Scuds. I called the Fighter Weapons School commander, Col L. D. Johnston, and talked to one of the test pilots who had dropped the munitions I recommended. I passed this detailed information to a Checkmate augmentee and to CENTAF. General Schwarzkopf commented a short time later on the immense value of "a neutralization strategy" which had helped keep the allied coalition intact.

A week into the air war, Colonel Litman organized a munitions effects assessment cell, largely made up of people from weapons labs and test centers from across the country. I began analyzing munitions effectiveness trends and studying potential targets for new weapons systems that were still being built. I helped provide our targeting analysis to a huge interagency effort toward successful employment of the "Deep Throat" (as Major General Ryan at TAC nicknamed it) penetrator against an Iraqi military command bunker. On 26 February, I briefed the TAC/IN, Colonel Minihan, who briefed General Russ, the TAC commander, on my ongoing analysis. However, the war was over the next day.

144

At this point, Colonel Litman formed a team of weapons effects engineers and structural engineers to fulfill CENTCOM's request for exploitation of bomb-damaged structures in Iraq and Kuwait. We operated under the Joint Captured Materiel Exploitation Center (JCMEC) (Rear) in Dhahran. We were the only official structural damage team to examine Iraqi bomb-damaged structures in detail.

At Norfolk Naval Air Station, we packed over 400 pounds of testing equipment into large cases and added them to our already large inventory of bulky camera equipment. The security guards at the passenger terminal helped us open the cases for inspection. The guards' faces turned from quizzical to aghast when they saw the rather large drills inside. Our 26 bags filled three-quarters of our aircraft's forward cargo hold.

Our trip lasted from 3 March to 17 March 1991, and it covered targets in Iraq and Kuwait. It included stops at Dhahran, Khafji, and King Khalid Military City (KKMC). We arrived at Riyadh Air Base, Saudi Arabia, some 20 hours after leaving Norfolk. We quickly settled into "Cabin Village," which became somewhat of a rear operating base for us. On 5 March we flew aboard a C-130 to King Khalid Military City just below the Saudi-Iraqi border, where we awaited transportation to Iraq. Unfortunately, the worst sandstorm of the year grounded us at KKMC until the following morning. After the sandstorm, the base resembled a ghost town out of the Old West. It was a desolate place. However, American humor was still evident in the "Yard of the Month" signs posted outside the tents. After waiting out the sandstorm for a day and a half, we finally flew on a CH-47 helicopter to Tallil airfield in Iraq. Our trip was a gold mine with regard to structural analysis, intelligence value, and unique items of interest.

As our helicopter hovered above the airfield, we saw the extent of the damage to the airfield's buildings and shelters. The devastation was breathtaking. Upon landing, USAF combat camera crews hustled out. They had only a few hours to take pictures of the scene. We temporarily camped out on two huge 25-ton doors blown off a double drive-through hardened aircraft shelter. We were anxious to start. The first thing we noticed was a barely recognizable Hip helicopter

145

smashed on the apron in front of the shelter, completely destroyed from the secondary explosion of its fuel tanks. We also saw undamaged Hind helicopters off in the distance as we quickly scanned the horizon. We climbed on top of a large shelter with the help of a cable. The view from the top of the shelter was spectacular. We could hear the clanging of sheet metal and the whistling of the wind. Off in the distance we saw 10-foot pieces of concrete hanging by a single rebar in front of severely damaged shelters. It was like looking down on a graveyard. Moreover, it was bizarre to be actually standing on one of the shelters I had weaponeered.

Soon, our eight-member group split up and we headed for opposite ends of the nearly mile-long runway. We caught up with explosive ordnance disposal (EOD) team members who were combing the airfield for unexploded ordnance. We could see that allied aircraft had done a good job seeding the airfield. Mines were everywhere. In fact, we figured out the Iraqis had developed home remedies for checking which mines were live. They tied long ropes to farm tractors' shift levers and guided them from a distance. We laughed at that. I began examining the insides of the hardened aircraft shelters. I noted that most were severely damaged and that many contained more than one aircraft. In some instances, we noted craters up to 20 feet deep inside the shelters. Lanyards, canisters, and fins lay nearby. Part of my job was to film our initial impressions on video. There was so much debris to walk over that we called the shaky film "America's Home Video."

After a long day of exploring this massive facility on foot, we decided to find a safe place to bed down for the night. Our helicopter took off without us after we told them we would take a calculated risk and stay another day or two to acquire even more information. By this time, late in the evening, a reddish haze had settled over the destroyed airfield from the setting sun and continual dust storms. In many ways we were reminded of a scene from an old "Star Trek" episode. Against this eerie backdrop, I hopped aboard a beat-up tank to talk to some "tankers." They eagerly related incidents from the battle for Tallil, which had taken place only a few days before. Mostly, I remember their anxious questions about how their effort was perceived in the States and their proud stories of children back home.

An Air-Delivered Mine

Inside a Hardened Aircraft Shelter

The Front Gate at Tallil Airfield

An RAF Tornado Ejection Seat

Hardened Aircraft Bunker

A Young "Tanker" at Tallil Airfield

Examining the Effects of a USAF-Delivered 2,000-Pound Bomb

A baby-faced lieutenant, a tank platoon commander from the Army's airborne infantry regiment occupying the airfield, invited us to bunk at a vehicle maintenance building. We were amazed at the youth of this lieutenant (22 years old) and his platoon. He expressed growing concern over the large number of mines in the area. Suddenly he received orders to "pull up stakes." After leaving us with an old Iraqi kerosene heater to keep us warm, he wished us luck. His platoon departed in a huge cloud of dust. That scene reminded me of a teenage parking lot hangout. The party was over, and the hot rods ripped away into the night. At that instant, I felt like a teenager: out after curfew, in a place I wasn't supposed to be.

We finally spent the night just down the road in an abandoned building with an Air Force EOD team. It was extremely cold that night, and we boarded up our hostel against unwanted intruders. An Army captain told us of rumors that the local citizens were up in arms, and the Army guards had heard continual gunfire.

The next morning we continued our exploitation work at the airfield. Soon, a C-130 landed and dozens of CENTCOM personnel walked out. The airfield was suddenly buzzing with American and British transport helicopters circling above. Apache attack helicopters landed to look closer at their enemy equivalent, the Hind gunship. I and three more of our team jumped into a jeep with CENTCOM personnel to examine facilities off-base. As we approached the main gate, we noted the statues and shrines dedicated to Saddam. Someone had knocked out a portion of the gate's stone wall, and we agreed the Iraqis did this so they could drag aircraft through the gate. According to a small CENTAF Black Hole team, Iraqi aircraft were seen camouflaged under palm trees a few miles down the road.

While examining one particular command building, I carefully eased through a jagged hole in a jammed, metal-plated door. Inside the room I saw rotting food and a personal photo of a senior Iraqi commander with Saddam. Apparently trapped inside the room while under bomb attack, this person frantically axed his way out of a metal door to freedom. I felt this was a dramatic indicator of the effect on personnel inside the building.

After this initial inspection, I walked outside the building. I was surprised to see three mud-covered Iraqi civilians. To our amazement, they were attempting to surrender to us! We told them this wasn't necessary. A CENTCOM Arabic interpreter told us their truck had broken down and they were looking for food. After some initial confusion and shouts of "Saddam . . . down! Down Saddam!", we put our 9mm's away and gave them all the MREs we could spare. After a long thank you, we continued to roam the base. We took cover behind hardened aircraft shelters as EOD personnel blew up some of the runways and taxiways. Finally, we joined CENTCOM personnel for a flight to Jalibah Airfield.

Jalibah was a desolate, alert-type base with few buildings other than some NATO-style hardened aircraft shelters and personnel bunkers. Here we saw more of the same: severe damage inside shelters and one-ton doors blown over 400 feet down the taxiway by USAF bombs. One of the EOD teams ran over a mine that destroyed the back axle of its HMMWV. Fortunately, no one was injured.

A Hardened Aircraft Shelter in Iraq

Iraqi Trench and Revetted Positions between Khafji and Kuwait City

Captured Iraqi Tank at Camp Freedom, Kuwait City

Reviewing Maps at Camp Freedom, Kuwait City

Bunking at Camp Freedom, Kuwait City

The next portion of our trip was slower. Safely back at Cabin Village in Riyadh, we now planned to assess facilities in recently retaken Kuwait. As a targeteer, I was very familiar with maps, and I made some which helped us on our drive into Kuwait. After the frustration of failing to get support from CENTCOM, we resorted to using our US Army team leader's credit card to rent two ostentatious-looking Ford LTDs for the road trip to the JCMEC (Rear) in Dhahran. We looked like the "Saturday Night Live" creation, the "Beverly Arabs." Our three DIA/Army Ranger troops were embarrassed to drive to a war zone like this; they ducked sheepishly at most checkpoints. At Dhahran, we swapped our vehicles for HMMWVs and pushed the more than 300 miles to Kuwait City the next morning (11 March). We drove slowly through the heavily battered town of Khafji. We wound our way through an obstacle course of destroyed roads, derelict Iraqi equipment, and Iraqi revetments as we came closer and closer to the hundreds of burning oil wells in the distance.

We reached Camp Freedom, near bomb-damaged Kuwait International Airport, just as the sun was setting into the oil-blackened sky. We stayed in a transformed warehouse with the JCMEC (Forward). As we drove through the gate, we passed captured Iraqi military vehicles on our right. I clambered inside an Iraqi ZSU-23-4 antiaircraft artillery vehicle and moved its guns up and down. That was a rare experience for an intelligence officer.

That night, inside our new headquarters, we planned the next day's assessment of Ahmad Al-Jabir Airfield and talked over various precautionary measures with US Army exploitation and EOD specialists. We also spoke with US Army interrogation specialists and Kuwaiti augmentees, who were busily debriefing shell-shocked Iraqi officers. The Iraqi POWs were amazed at the precision of US air power and surprised at their humane treatment by their allied captors.

On March 12, we drove to Ahmad Al-Jabir Airfield with another team from Air Force Systems Command in our two HMMWVs. The airfield was occupied by British ground forces. They were conducting live-fire drills with captured Iraqi AAA guns in what we regarded as a courteous welcome salute. Again, helicopters hovered overhead as crew members recorded the overwhelming damage to the shelters and

155

buildings below. The British were still celebrating the news of the official cease-fire with a picnic and three-legged races. In a time-honored tradition, the allies traded MREs and shared a spot of tea. "Your MREs are better than ours, but not by much," the British soldiers joked. Initially, we decided the Kuwaiti aircraft bunkers were harder than those we had seen in Iraq and the damage from our attacks was not as severe. At any rate, they did not contain aircraft like those in Iraq. On the whole, however, allied aircraft hit the air-fields in Kuwait hard, and there was widespread damage.

On 13 March, we drove through vast, burning oil fields to another air base southwest of Kuwait City. It was a scene straight out of Dante's *Inferno*. Oil at times flowed like a river, 16 inches deep across the road. Fires blazed relentlessly on all sides. In both HMMWVs, the lower ranking officers were sitting in the open-back cabs. At one point, our lead vehicle's driver became disoriented and stopped. The swirling black smoke from the fires on all sides of us was so thick we could barely see the vehicle 20 feet ahead of us. I could feel the fire's heat on my helmet as I sat in the back of the second HMMWV. We told the team leader the maps were correct and we should "press ahead" even though it was difficult to see where we were going. Many of us thought our "shortcut" could have been fatal. This was the worst of a 20-mile abyss where we had not seen a single moving vehicle. We were surprised when we came through the wall of black smoke into a clear sky.

Ahmad Al-Jabir was one of the most dangerous facilities we assessed. The majority of the bomblets had not been cleared by coalition teams. A Marine captain we met said he would not even let his own EOD teams operate off the main runways and perimeter roads. He loaned us a guide, who was helpful.

We departed the airfield early in the afternoon and made our way north to the infamous "Highway of Death" where Iraqi columns were battered by fierce air attacks—ultimately driving the president's termination of hostilities. What we saw was a definitive statement on the whole conflict—miles of death and destruction inflicted on Iraqi "looters" frantically fleeing the scene of the crime. Kuwaiti citizens now joined many groups of soldiers from several nations, gaping in

156

An Oil Well Fire Near Kuwait City

Driving through Oil Well Fires in Kuwait

Ahmad Al-Jabir Airfield, Kuwait

Team Leaders at Ahmad Al-Jabir Airfield

North to Basra

awe at this powerful image. Tractor-trailers hauling armored personnel carriers (APC) had run into each other, many tanks were completely scorched, and scores of stolen Kuwaiti domestic vehicles gushed masses of clothing and personal effects.

That evening, we visited downtown Kuwait City for the first time. Clearly, this had been a beautiful city at one time. Even with its tall, swaying palm trees, however, the city looked completely trashed from fires, small arms, and mortar fire. I sat outside the only downtown hotel that had electricity while I waited for our team leader, who was meeting with the US Army Corps of Engineers inside. A Kuwaiti couple approached me, looking for water. I promptly gave them some of our ration, and they handed me a small Kuwaiti flag in exchange. Everywhere we went, Kuwaiti flags, smiles, honking horns, and victory signs greeted us.

On our way back to Camp Freedom, we passed a large telecommunications tower and a control building that appeared damaged. We tried to enter the building, but a Kuwaiti soldier kept us out. We noted

A Precision Bomb "Hit" in Kuwait City

the incredible precision of US bombs. There were only a few holes in select windows, with little other observable damage on the exterior. We proceeded along the road to Camp Freedom and, just as on preceding days, we passed Kuwaiti children running to the roadside looking for food. This time we threw them a whole box of MREs, which they quickly dragged away. We smiled in a moment of joy mixed with just a tinge of relief. We never liked dehydrated peaches.

The next morning, we visited Ash Shuwaykh Port Facility and Ras Al Qualayah Naval Base. At the port facility, we saw several large gantry cranes toppled into the water. Upon closer examination, we found wires leading to a blast-cap box in the water. We pulled the box out of the water, noted the "MOD Baghdad" label, and concluded that the Iraqis had blown up the cranes shortly before leaving the port. This was another example of their wanton destruction of Kuwaiti facilities. As we drove down the coast to Ras Al Qualayah, we noted the scores of US Navy cluster munitions canisters littering the roadsides south of the base.

Once inside the naval base, we observed the dry-dock area, which was almost completely destroyed as were several surrounding buildings. We also closely examined large Iraqi AAA pieces sitting out on the piers. We met an Australian EOD team at the base, and we asked them if they would like to sit down to an MRE or make a trade. They were too smart for that. We soon departed Kuwait on an abnormally sunny day. At the Kuwait-Saudi border, we passed scores of Kuwaiti transport trucks and vehicles crammed along the road heading north. We started down the coastal highway south to Dhahran.

On 17 March, most of our team returned home to the United States. I stayed behind because I hoped to collect more damage exploitation data and because I wanted to debrief General Horner on our initial assessments. He was very pleased with our effort, and we exchanged ideas on the success of various aircraft and munitions during the war. He told me the story behind various air attacks, which helped our later analysis.

The following day an L-1011 took me home. One of the trip's highlights was the 500 people of all ages who met the plane at 5:00 A.M. in Bangor, Maine. Elderly women handed out cookies, veterans

An Iraqi-Destroyed Kuwaiti Crane

Ras Al Qualayah Naval Base

Ali Al Salem Air Base

View from Atop a Hardened Aircraft Bunker at Ali Al Salem Air Base, Kuwait

shook our hands, and kids thanked us for doing a good job. I felt somewhat undeserving of this tumultuous welcome, yet I felt proud to have played a small part in this historic eight-month effort.

Lessons Learned

Based on my experience in Desert Storm, I've made the following observations/conclusions.

1. We hear time and time again, "intelligence failed." USAF leaders should be more discriminating in their approach—it shouldn't be a shotgun blast. If we don't answer how and why "it failed," then we can't remedy the problem. Instead of merely cataloging intelligence failures, we must characterize these mistakes in a precise and objective manner. I think we can expect mistakes from intelligence analysts just as we can expect mistakes from planners and pilots. This is a natural phenomenon during war, especially a war conducted at the rate of Desert Storm. We need to move beyond the simple catch-all indictments. We need to look more at where targeting (the intersection of intelligence and combat operations) failed.

2. Intelligence as a whole can't take the cautious approach it did during Desert Shield. The intelligence community has to be an *active* participant in the war-planning process; otherwise, unobjective and unqualified rated staffs will try to do the job. Then everyone loses. Pilots will have to reattack targets on which we previously overestimated bomb damage (the result of wishful thinking or hidden agendas), and thousands of dollars spent training our intelligence specialists will be squandered. We need some degree of caution and objectivity in intelligence analysis, but we also need people who are outgoing and aggressive enough to push pertinent information to combat planners. Granted, these are hard qualities to find, especially during these times. Few are willing to take chances with career advancement.

3. The major problem with intelligence support during Desert Storm was not production but distribution. National-level intelligence agencies can't just turn out mission-planning products, then ignore how they are used by theater commands and combat units. We can't

afford to take the attitude that "once the materials go out of the building, we can't worry about where they end up." We need a good solid "hand-off" to intelligence consumers, and we need fast feedback. We should develop well-trained intelligence community "salesmen" to travel along with the planning products, collect instant face-to-face feedback with disparate consumers and then return to Washington, feedback in hand.

4. During Desert Storm, there was a shortage of qualified targeting officers, both in-theater and in Washington. This will only be exacerbated in the future, with the ongoing force reductions, and a critical situation will only be made worse.

Finally, during Desert Storm, some USAF captains, along with senior officers, no doubt, were content to "be there." They managed to stay "on the sidelines, out of harm's way." Most, however, often without regard for career and sometimes without regard for life, stepped up to the historic challenge. Along these lines, a good credo for all junior officers to follow in future conflicts might be "Everything is my job." My experiences not only reinforced many of the principles stressed time and time again in our USAF training, such as honor, duty, country; they also gave meaning to these and other principles. For example, I learned firsthand about real leadership, and the importance of this sometimes transparent quality in overcoming the fog and friction of war. We have heard many lectures on leadership in our PME training as company grade officers. However, we were able to see leadership in action in Desert Storm, and we now know that it comes in many forms. Furthermore, some of us became the types of leaders we had studied in the past but somehow never thought we were capable of being.

*   *   *

This article is dedicated to the memory of a former A-10 squadron mate and friend, Captain Stephen Phillis, killed in action during Operation Desert Storm.

Crusade against Tyranny

by

Capt Greg Eanes

For me, the war was a crusade against tyranny. I left my position as a staff instructor at Goodfellow AFB's Intelligence Training Center on 11 August 1990. After 13 years in the military, I knew internally that we were going to liberate Kuwait, one way or another, before I came home again. One of the last things I remember telling my wife was that I would be home when Kuwait was free. From that point on, I devoted my efforts to doing what I could to help win the war.

People say that Desert Shield was not a "war." That's hogwash. There's a certain mind-set that we must assume in such situations so the ultimate goal is never forgotten. Mentally, physically, and emotionally, I was personally at war with Iraq. That is the mind-set I had to assume in order to keep the various tasks and the ultimate mission in mind. Desert Shield was the preparation phase of the war, but it ended only when all the pockets of Iraqi resistance in Kuwait City capitulated many days after the armistice was declared.

I did everything I possibly could to support the SOCCENT mission. I've never limited myself to being a "specialist." I try to know a little about everything so I can contribute in emergencies. This has given me a well-rounded background, though not always one with depth in regards to certain functions. I cannot abide the "It's-not-my-job" attitude. My philosophy has always been, "If it needs to be done and you know how to do it, it's your job." Consequently, I served a number of functions within the SOCJ2. At one time, I was working or assisting in all the intelligence functional areas. This was not because I was a specialist, but because I had some knowledge and I was willing to risk attempting to do whatever had to be done. In the beginning we were tremendously undermanned, and we were augmented with personnel who had no background in joint or special operations. We also had little or no systems support, which frustrated people accustomed to working with quality high tech systems. My background, training, and sense of duty personally obligated me to attempt every task regardless of personal consequences.

Working with the Kuwaiti resistance was very meaningful. Hearing firsthand the accounts of Iraqi atrocities only served to strengthen my own resolve. I kept a photo of a four-year-old Kuwaiti girl who was among a group of refugees that escaped around late September. Only moments before the picture was taken, she was with her mother, baby brother, and other refugees. The baby brother, sitting on the mother's lap, held a Kuwaiti flag, which was illegal. The Iraqi penalty was death. The Iraqis took the mother and the baby and let the rest go. If the Iraqi soldiers followed their standard practice, the mother would have been brutally raped and beaten before she was killed, but not before she witnessed the murder of her own baby. In the picture, the little girl flashes the "V" for victory sign while appearing to hold back a great emotional outburst. She reflects an aura of fear, defiance, and hope. I looked into her eyes and could not help but share the emotion. I could not help but think of my own wife and daughters (about the same age) and feel a burning rage. The atrocity stories are well documented. Kuwait was subjected to a holocaust. There's no doubt in my mind that we did the right thing. Witnessing the smiling faces and crammed streets on liberation day was proof of that.

In October, our first SOCJ2 became very sick, so the primary targets officer and deputy SOCJ2, a Navy lieutenant commander, carried his duties. Due to low manning and the fact that I'd been working targeting issues with him since late September, I was appointed acting chief of targets. In this capacity, I helped coordinate the initial intelligence collection and targeting efforts on the first two targets struck in the war—Iraqi early warning sites. We looked at these targets and weapon systems within the special operations community from a variety of ways. Eventually, some 101st Aviation Brigade helicopters were chopped to Air Force Special Operations Command. They executed the mission after being led into the target area by USAF SOF (AFSOC) helicopters. In my opinion, the real credit for much of

A Kuwaiti Soldier Describes His Family

the detailed planning must go to a targeteer by the name of Capt Bob Jayme. "Targeteer Bob" was a prior enlisted intelligence officer who knew how the system worked and also knew how to "work the system." More than one piece of intelligence came our way through Bob's wheeling and dealing in Riyadh and elsewhere. Utilizing natural cunning and other skills, Bob put together an outstanding package for special operators early in the crisis. In addition to his important work, his wry sense of humor helped me keep everything in the proper perspective. That alone was worth all the system support in the world.

We received a large influx of people in the October/November time frame, which allowed us to reallocate jobs. By the second week of December, I had begun focusing on my responsibilities as SOCCENT evasion and escape (E & E) officer. (SOCCENT was the CENTCOM executive agent for combat search and rescue operations and evasion and escape operations.) I served as the single point of contact for the entire theater regarding E & E matters. My E & E duties were most

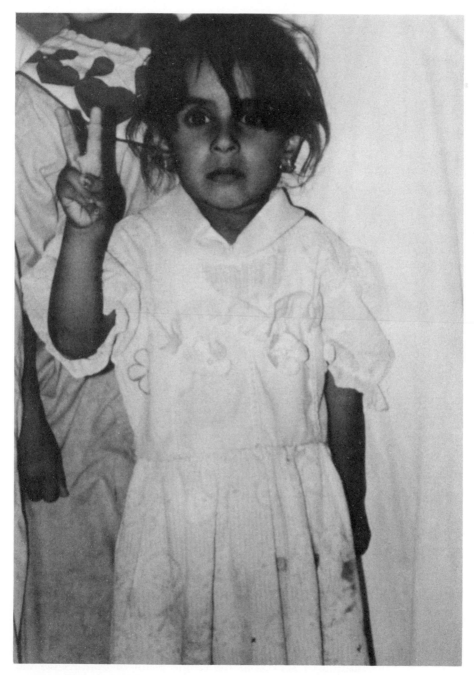

Victory, of Sorts, for a Young Kuwaiti Girl

rewarding. My experience at SOCEUR, as a Navy SERE (survival, evasion, resistance to interrogation) instructor and a student of history, prepared me for the E & E challenges of this war. Using the operations order (1002-90) as my charter and World War II E & E history as my primary guide, I worked to fulfill our E & E responsibilities for the entire CENTCOM theater. I didn't do it alone, however. There were numerous people back in the States, at various agencies, that helped us get valuable intelligence products after we identified and defined what we needed. There was also some help in-theater.

As the SOCCENT E & E officer, I coordinated the program, and did all the legwork, that produced the "blood chits" for all US and British forces during Desert Storm. I also ensured that the intelligence community studied and created corridors for the aircrews to use during evasion. I was an intermediary between the conventional forces and the resistance forces that prepared to help the evasion and escape effort once the war started. (At least one "save" was partially due to the blood chits.)

Finally, I arrived in Kuwait City with the SOCCENT advance convoy on 28 February, or "victory in the Gulf (VG) day" as the Saudis called it. We had travelled all day on the 27th, and we camped out at a depot that night on the border. It was cold, wet, drizzling, and muddy. We heard a BBC rebroadcast of President Bush's declaration of a cease-fire to take effect at 0800 our time. It was good news, but we still had work to do.

Going through the breach, we were able to see the Iraqi mine fields, destroyed enemy tanks, the fire pits, and bunker systems. Marines were along the sides of the road at various places. Even at 1000, the sky was pitch-black with smoke from the burning oil fires. The cold weather accentuated the heat from the fires, and the hissing sound of burning oil wells was the only thing we could hear. There was no other noise. If you could picture Dante's *Inferno*, this had to be it. Just north of Ahmad Al-Jabir Airfield, our convoy was stopped. Approximately 150 Iraqis who had been bypassed by the Marines emerged from their bunker complex and were ready to fight. There was an exchange of fire between them and the Marines.

Marine artillery pounded the Iraqis and they were given 45 minutes to surrender. They surrendered.

Entering Kuwait City reminded me of the newsreel footage of the liberation of Paris. People were in the streets laughing, yelling, and flashing the victory sign. At one point, we stopped our truck so I could run out and give some children a shoe box full of candy and gum I had brought specifically for the occasion. I figured they could use some treats by this time. Their broad smiles and frantic waves told me it was appreciated.

We finally met up with our follow-on element, which had been airlifted that afternoon. We encamped at the Kuwaiti air defense base. The next day, we established three teams (each with five Kuwaitis and five Americans) so we could begin collecting evidence of Iraqi war crimes. Though we searched many buildings, a portion of my team focused on a 12-gun artillery site situated on an old dirt racetrack. The battery commander's bunker was a mother lode of documents. We pulled out nine large crates of documents concerning a whole range of operations, including occupation duty requirements, arrest and desertion records, and a signed order from Saddam Hussein directing his battery commanders to use chemical weapons when the Americans showed up. I also recovered a large Ba'ath Party flag from this bunker. The documents indicated the officer was probably a Ba'ath Party member. Another team found what appeared to be a torture chamber, one of many that would be discovered by combined Kuwaiti and American teams. There was even a skating rink where one soldier described the bodies of torture victims "stacked like cordwood." These discoveries did not dampen the joy of the Kuwaiti people, though. Every night for weeks, the strand in front of the western embassies was overflowing with joyful celebration. The Kuwaiti holocaust was finally over.

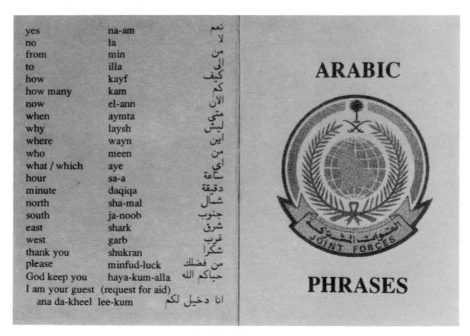

yes	na-am	نعم
no	la	لا
from	min	من
to	illa	الى
how	kayf	كيف
how many	kam	كم
now	el-ann	الان
when	aymta	متى
why	laysh	ليش
where	wayn	اين
who	meen	من
what / which	aye	اي
hour	sa-a	ساعة
minute	daqiqa	دقيقة
north	sha-mal	شمال
south	ja-noob	جنوب
east	shark	شرق
west	garb	غرب
thank you	shukran	شكرا
please	minfud-luck	من فضلك
God keep you	haya-kum-alla	حياكم الله
I am your guest	(request for aid)	
	ana da-kheel lee-kum	انا دخيل لكم

Arabic Phrases

173

RATED OFFICERS

Desert Rescue

by

Capt Paul Johnson

My comments are recorded here for two reasons. First, I think it's important that we operators—I refer to captains as operators because we're there when the rubber meets the road—understand that our doctrine, our training, our equipment, and our command, control, and communications don't always work well. I also want you to understand that Paul Johnson did not execute a rescue mission in Desert Storm—it was a large effort, a team effort. This is a war story with lessons learned.

As my A-10 squadron at Myrtle Beach, South Carolina, prepared to deploy to Southwest Asia, my squadron commander called me into his office and told me, "We're going to Saudi Arabia and you're not." He kicked me out the door and sent me to Fighter Weapons School at Nellis. I thought I had died; it hurt! As it turned out, I missed almost all of Desert Shield. I arrived at King Fahd International Airport, about 30 miles north of Dhahran, on New Year's Eve. In addition to King Fahd, we had a forward-operating location (FOL) at King Khalid Military City (KKMC). Finally, when we started reacting to the Scud attacks, we sent some A-10s out to a place called Al Jouk, which we referred to as the "wild, wild west." We flew Scud reconnaissance throughout the war.

Although many people think of the A-10 as a close-air-support weapon, we flew very little close air support. We did a great deal of battlefield air interdiction, however. Our concept of operation emphasized working in Kuwait and the tri-border area. Our targets were to be infantry, armor, and artillery; and we were to kill Iraqis on the battlefield with any ordnance we could. We knew where the artillery was, where the Republican Guard was, where the Hammurabi was, and where the Nebuchadnezzar was. We knew which divisions were in which positions. We did not know much about what was going on in the west because we planned to go to war in the east. We were also sitting search and rescue (SAR) alert. We had two airplanes sitting alert on the ground at King Fahd and two airplanes sitting alert on the ground at KKMC. We wound up doing a lot of Scud search, but that wasn't in the original plan.

On 21 January Randy Goff and I were supposed to go to KKMC to sit SAR alert. About the time we woke up that morning, an EA-6 Prowler from the USS *Saratoga* was flying into central Iraq, escorted by Lts Devon Jones and Larry Slade in an F-14 Tomcat. At about 0530, the Prowler put a high-speed antiradiation missile into a radar sight at an Iraqi airfield in prelude to an attack. A SAM hit the F-14 during the attack, forcing Devon and Larry to eject into darkness at 14,000 feet. They lost contact with each other.

Tom Trask and his Pave Low crew (Moccasin 05) were the first to begin the rescue effort. Flying at 100 feet, they started looking for Slate 46 (Jones and Slade) early in the morning, using the terrain-following radar to overcome the low visibility and ground fog. I have the highest respect for this airplane, the men who fly it, and their capabilities. Because they were initially told that the survivors were well south of their eventual location, they and Enfield (A-10s that had been searching for Scuds) searched in vain. Enfield searched up high for Slate 46 on the radio, while Moccasin searched down low. Neither had any luck.

Meanwhile Randy Goff and I waited at King Fahd for favorable weather so we could go to KKMC. Finally under way, we were diverted west to aid in the search. We coordinated for a tanker and finally refueled, although the thunderstorms and clouds almost forced us back to KKMC. After we refueled from the KC-135, we called Yukon (AWACS), who was coordinating everything, and said we were ready to go. Yukon told us that, so far, no one had had any luck. The helicopter had to refuel, and it hadn't made contact. Enfield hadn't made contact and had returned to search for Scuds. Yukon then told us to check out a possible Scud sighting. In my mind, the rescue had just fallen on its face. After 90 minutes of searching to the southeast, we determined there were no Scuds and left the Bedouins alone in their tents. When we needed to refuel again, the KC-10 ("Tuna") refueled us. At this point I thought we would be heading back to the FOL because the rescue attempt was over. Instead, Yukon sent us back to search for the known survivor. I expected a fruitless search.

Randy and I headed out "tapline road" and started our search, again to the southwest of Baghdad. We kept wondering what we were doing deep inside Iraq with little idea as to what kind of threat we faced. The weather was good in Iraq. We tried to tiptoe inconspicuously at 15,000 feet. Fortunately, there wasn't much of anything out there—but we didn't know that. We began searching, and we began calling, "Slate 46 this is Sandy 57, Slate 46 this is Sandy 57." We searched in the area where we were told he was supposed to be, but we had absolutely no luck.

Meanwhile, Devon Jones was on the ground. He never made contact with Larry Slade. He tried to head west, but when the sun came up in his face, he realized he was disoriented. He headed south until midmorning when he found vegetation in some low hills and decided to burrow in and hide.

We were about 10 minutes from having to abandon the search for lack of fuel, when Devon Jones answered our call. "Slate 46 this is Sandy 57." "Sandy this is Slate, go ahead." I was flabbergasted; he answered! "Slate this is Sandy 57. How do you read?" "Sandy, this is Slate. Loud and clear." I thought, "Boy, you're a calm fellow for somebody who jumped out of an airplane in the middle of the night." At this point, I tried to authenticate him because some search and rescue forces in Southeast Asia were drawn into traps through the radios—and he seemed awfully calm on the radio. Yukon radioed for some personal information, and we ascertained that this was not only an American, but that this was Devon Jones, the front seater of an F-14 Tomcat flying off the USS *Saratoga*.

Then we had to find out where he was. We used some equipment that was supposed to give me a directional steer to where his signal was coming from, the exact same equipment they used in Southeast Asia 25 years ago. The signal was so weak that I couldn't get any

179

directional steers; all I could get was voice. At this point, I became very scientific. From a beginning point, I began flying west while talking to Devon. When the signal faded, I realized that wasn't right. I returned to my starting point and began heading east until the signal faded. That wasn't right. I returned again to my starting point and began heading north. As the signal became stronger, the directional steer pointed further north into Iraq. "Great," I thought facetiously, "that's just what I wanted to see." Although I knew I was headed in the right direction, I had no idea how far north I had to fly. I kept thinking it will be 10 miles farther up, or 15 miles farther up. By the time we located Devon Jones, we were roughly due west of Baghdad! Fortunately, my map was folded so I couldn't see just how close I was to Baghdad. Ignorance really is bliss.

As I headed toward Devon, he had no idea who I was. Flying in and out of scattered puffy clouds, I often couldn't see the ground—and Devon couldn't see me. When I was close to where I thought he was, I flew down below the clouds and popped out some very bright self-protection flares (they are usually used for protection against infrared missiles). Devon spotted one of these and began vectoring me toward his position. Although I was only 200 or 300 feet above him, I didn't see him. He told me when I was overhead, and I marked the spot with my inertial navigation system (INS). I then climbed and tried to memorize the terrain features: a couple of dirt tracks crossing each other, a blue tank off to the side, some vegetation that someone had tried to cultivate once upon a time. I memorized the scene and I knew that when I saw the scene again, I would find Devon.

Unfortunately, gas, which had been short when I initially talked to Devon on the radio, was now critically short. The last thing I wanted to do to a survivor was leave him, but I had to leave for fuel. If I had been Devon, I would have taken out my pistol and shot at me. Devon said, "Fine. Talk to you when you get back." I thought he was a very calm fellow all day long. I don't know that he had much choice. He may have said some choice words after he left the radio.

As we headed south, we began trying to put things together. First, I told Yukon to turn the tanker north. Yukon either missed this call or ignored it, and said, "Roger, your tanker is vector 165 for 150." I said,

"No, Yukon. Turn the tanker north, now." Tuna turned north. Tom Trask in the Pave Low, who had been at a refueling location just over the border, was listening to what we were saying. Although he hadn't heard Devon, he heard some of what I said and a lot of what Yukon said. When he found out we found Devon, the first thing he wanted to know was Devon's location. While I was southbound, I passed the location information on to Tom.

Unfortunately, inertial navigation systems, especially single INSs, tend to drift. Since mine had been drifting for about five hours now, it was only accurate enough to keep me someplace in Iraq. I passed the information on to Tom, but I knew it wasn't accurate. Tom wasn't about to wait on me, and he began moving northeast with what he had. If I had crashed and burned, Tom would have gone on without me. I didn't want any MiG-29s or other Iraqi aircraft poking their noses into my business, so I asked Yukon for some combat air patrol (CAP). Yukon coordinated with a flight of F-15s, who began flying toward us. I also asked if Enfield was still airborne, but the A-10s were too far south to effect the rescue.

The second most beautiful sight of the day was a big beautiful KC-10 coming north to meet me inside Iraq. Late in the war, tankers could touch-and-go in Baghdad if they wanted, but this KC-10 was at 15,000 feet, 30 miles inside Iraq, on the fifth day of the war. I called that a save, since we had only 1,500 pounds of fuel. As soon as we filled our tanks and dropped off the boom, the KC-10 scooted back across the border.

At this point everyone was headed north. Moccasin was headed northeast, and we were trying to catch him as fast as we could. The F-15s called, "Sandy, this is Texaco, where do you want us?" I directed them right over Devon to protect us. Although I would've preferred to stay above the clouds so as not to highlight Moccasin, Randy and I dropped down below the clouds to escort Moccasin in a "daisy chain" pattern.

The radios then went out of control. Because I knew my INS fix on Devon was inaccurate, I began talking to him on the radio to refine his position. Simultaneously I had to vector the Pave Low toward Devon, since Tom had the old, inaccurate INS position. Additionally,

I had to coordinate our escort with Randy and Tom. To top it all off, Texaco began talking to Yukon about how to orient the CAP and who would point his radar in which direction. Finally I said, "Everyone but Slate, Moccasin, and Sandy, shut up." That was not good radio discipline, but you could've heard a pin drop. Texaco and Yukon probably worked things out on another frequency.

Finally, things came together. Devon and Moccasin, the survivor and the helicopter, finally made radio contact. Devon saw Moccasin and began vectoring him. I finally saw the scene I had memorized when I first found Devon, and I thought, "OK, I've been here before." Then somebody saw a fast-moving truck heading toward Devon. I said, "Slate, confirm the truck is headed in your general direction." He said, "The truck is headed straight for me." "OK," I thought, "take the truck." When Randy and I rolled in, I had little confidence that it was a military truck. Randy still believes it was not a military truck. He thought it was what we called a water truck, going out to supply animals, or farms, or homes. He thought it was some farmer who was lost. Devon is convinced beyond a shadow of a doubt that it was an Iraqi military truck. It didn't matter. We had two hogs, we had a survivor on the ground, we had a 50-million dollar Pave Low with people on board. I'm sorry, wrong place, wrong time. To this day, I don't know if I killed one poor Iraqi farmer or 15 Iraqi grunts sitting in the back seat. The truck ate 30-millimeter ammunition, and the gas tank exploded. Nobody who was there has any regrets.

While we were shooting the truck, Tom circled the Pave Low to stay clear of the area. After we shot the truck, Devon stood up while Tom air-taxied over to him. Randy and I went into a "hover-cover," orbiting the area. The scene was reminiscent of Southeast Asia. Devon ran over to the helicopter, and we headed south.

We had to cross a major highway as we escorted Moccasin to the border. I asked Moccasin if he wanted to shoot across or sneak across, and he said we should find a gap and sneak across. I peeled off to the west, Randy drifted east, Tom slowed down, and we scooted through a gap in the traffic. I've often wondered what some poor Iraqi truck driver thought, seeing an American Pave Low motoring across the highway, 20 feet off the deck at high noon on the fifth day of the war: "The war is lost, the war is lost."

We escorted Tom southwest in the shortest direction to the border until we found some familiar terrain. We asked Moccasin if they were good to go, and he said, "We've got it from here." Randy and I headed south for our fourth refueling of the day. Tuna met us on the north side of the border. After refueling, we started the 90-minute trip home. We had refueled four times in almost nine hours of flying. A few days later, Devon was back on the *Saratoga* flying missions in the war.

It takes a big team to make a rescue happen. We estimate about 50 for this rescue. Also, the backup helicopters and the Enfield A-10s were as capable as we were, and they would have done the job if they had been there.

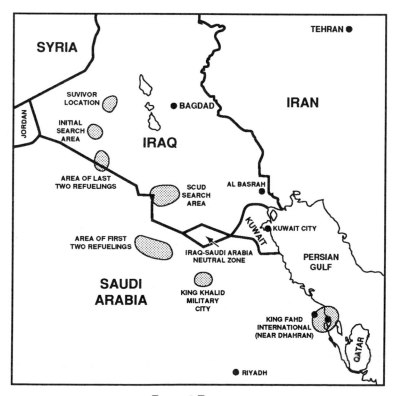

Desert Rescue

Lessons

Although Pave Low drivers customarily think of nighttime, single-ship rescues, Moccasin did none of that with us. Nobody will go to war exactly as they plan; and if they expect to, they will be awakened rudely.

Hopefully, our doctrine will drive our training. The problem is that doctrine may be missing, wrong, or vague. We use doctrine to build a training system, a command and control system, a set of tactics, and so forth. Sometimes it doesn't work. Tom used a Pave Low in a way he hadn't planned. The KC-10 didn't plan on being in Iraq. Ken Mulligan in the AWACS, accustomed to handling air-to-air engagements between high-speed fighters, was instead serving as a communication relay coordinator for a couple of hogs and a helicopter. Everyone did things they didn't expect to do, and they did them extremely well.

Let me use search and rescue as an example for discussing our doctrine and our training. I'll pull no punches. For those of us who trained in SAR, the instructions in the air tasking order were a joke. In many ways, search and rescue command, control, and communications were broken. We did excellent work in Desert Storm, but let's not break our arms while we pat ourselves on the back. Not everything went the way we would have liked it to go. But if it's broken—be it training; doctrine; command, control, and communications; or whatever—we operators get to pick up the pieces.

We're the ones who have to pick up what's there, put it together, and try to make it work. On 21 January 1991, that's exactly what we did. We put together a scratch team, everybody brought something to the party, everyone trusted in the skills of the people that were there to do their jobs, and we pulled it off. Nobody balked because we all knew why we were there that day.

Code Name	Cast of Characters	Aircraft
Slate 46	Lt Devon Jones, pilot	F-14
	Lt Larry Slade, radar intercept officer	
Moccasin 05	Capt Tom Trask, pilot	Pave Low
Moccasin 06		Backup
Yukon	Capt Ken Mulligan, primary controller	AWACS
Tuna		KC-10 tanker
Texaco		F-15
Enfield		A-10
Sandy 57	Capt Paul Johnson	A-10
Sandy 58	Capt Randy Goff	A-10

Through the Eyes of a Buff Driver

by

Capt Paul J. Moscarelli

On 16 January 1991, I arrived in Jeddah, Saudi Arabia, for what were to be the two most interesting and introspective months of my life. These excerpts from the journal I kept during Operation Desert Storm document the emotional roller coaster I experienced. I hope you can share my anticipation, fear, rage, boldness, homesickness, and pride.

Saudi Arabia, 1530, 17 January 1991. I am sitting on a cot in the facility normally used by Moslems on a pilgrimage to Mecca. Tom Thompson is on the other side of the 12-person room, assembling a chemical warfare mask while the BBC reporter on the radio exclaims, "The Iraqis have underestimated the ferocity of the American response!"

I've been awake since 0100. I had trouble sleeping (anticipation, jet lag). A KC-135 crew chief told me, "It's started." His eyes were wide open. He was obviously highly charged with adrenaline. We walked up on the roof and looked out over the ramp. Almost all of the 85 tankers that were there when we went to sleep had vanished. The crew chief, still gazing wide-eyed out over the ramp, said, "I worked my usual 12-hour shift, then they made me come back to go to sleep. I wanted to keep working, but they wouldn't let me—said I had to rest up for my next shift."

I've only been here for a day, but my thinking has changed. I'm astounded at what I've seen here. The US military, normally the most inefficient of bureaucracies, is operating like a well-oiled machine. The ability of these people to close ranks and do the job is reflected in everything, from planning strike missions down to the food in the chow hall. Everything is done correctly and on time. Simply amazing!

The men on our crews are optimistic, although a couple are obviously very worried. Jokes and insults fly freely—it's almost like being at camp. But faces become sober when the conversation turns to home—how afraid our wives and families must be, and how much easier this is for us than for them.

My 11 roomies went to breakfast, and I'm alone. The first B-52s are landing now. Maintenance troops stand by to load new weapons and fuel for the next attack. President Bush is talking on the radio, presenting what I'm sure will be called his "while the world stood by" speech. Eric Single walks in and offers me a laundry bag. Apparently, we are being provided professional laundry service—definitely not something I expected when I marched off to war. It's time for breakfast.

2100, 17 January 1991. Aircraft activity is picking up. Six B-52s went to deliver a message—240,000 pounds of high explosives—to the Iraqi Republican Guard. How long will they stand up to this kind of firepower? I spent the morning on the ramp, moving airplanes back and forth from fuel loading to munitions loading. It felt good to be contributing a little. It's funny how emotions run through peaks and valleys. Hearts sank when only five of the six B-52s reported in after the first strike, but smiles were ear-to-ear when number six appeared, unannounced and with broken radios, on final approach. Waves of patriotism hit me for the tiniest reasons, like driving by the rows of tankers and seeing all the state names painted on the tails—"Kansas, Illinois, New Hampshire, Alaska." When I think about the people and the places we call America, and how great they are, a tear comes to my eye.

I took a nap in the afternoon. Everyone is still battling jet lag. Some of the guys slept most of the day—obviously not seasoned travelers. (You have to fight jet lag, not sleep it away.)

We feel the threat of terrorism here. Our compound seems relatively secure, but the buses that shuttle us back and forth are fitted with curtains so that we cannot be identified and there is no opportunity for a clear shot at us. As I ran along the perimeter of the compound tonight, it occurred to me that the palm trees across the road would provide excellent cover for a sniper. I retreated within the inner walls.

2315, 17 January. I was just notified of a 1715 show tomorrow. That means we'll fly at night. I'm comfortable with that. Darkness is our element, not theirs. Sleep will not come easily tonight. I think I'll sew the hole in my flight suit.

0910, 18 January. I slept a couple of hours last night. I'll probably get some more this afternoon. That seems to be when I'm most tired. My crew's reaction to the news that we were flying tonight ranged from bloodthirsty elation to abject fear. Some went to bed and snored like a buzz saw for nine hours. I answered a letter from an eight-year-old girl in Wisconsin. I told her about B-52s and the names of our gerbils. I'm sure her class will enjoy the letter. I hope I can sleep.

2223, Airborne over Saudi. Everything felt normal up to this point. Preflight, takeoff, and climb out were no big deal. Saudi air defense threatened to shoot us down for flying too close to Mecca. Now we're leveled off with plenty of time to think. My stomach feels funny. Maybe I'm just hungry. I'll try to eat something. The desert is black as coal.

0100, 19 January. Homeward bound. I didn't know my heart could beat that fast. That was easily the most frightening experience of my life. The most frightening thing of all was that we were completely unprepared to do what we did. We had no clue what it would really be like. Missiles and AAA were flying around. There was crap all over the radios. Friendly fighters rolled in behind us. I feel better now. We will be better next time. The crew will communicate better and exchange the necessary information. Thank God for F-4G Wild Weasels—they saved us! As we turned toward the target, I felt kind of bad about dropping on the Iraqis; but once they tried to kill me, those feelings faded. We'll see them again soon.

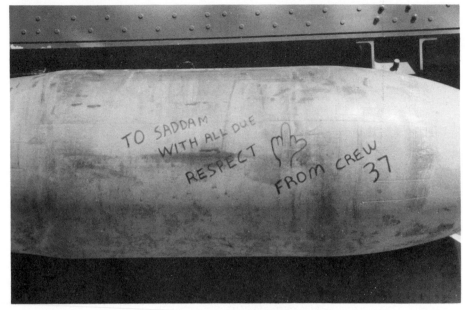

To Saddam, with All Due Respect

Messengers from the Sky

High Above the Earth

0000, 20 January. It's really kind of fun to be here. I remember my instructor when I was learning to be a copilot, saying, "Vietnam was really pretty fun. The only problem was that you could get killed." There are lots of jokes, excitement, cursing, volleyball games, and "there I was" stories. When we were notified that bus time was in 30 minutes, briefing in an hour, takeoff in four, my heart started racing and the mood turned deadly serious.

The room was silent. I reminded my crew of the lessons we learned and how we're going to do it right tonight. We threw our gear together, walked out the door, and headed for the bus stop. At this point, you could probably have extracted a quart of adrenaline from our veins.

An airman walked over to me and handed me a note that said, "mission canceled." I read the note to the 18 guys standing around with their bags in their hands. There was instantaneous relaxation. Some guys started complaining, others cursed, and others joked. I joked a lot. I did everything I could to keep the mood light.

191

Oh yes, remember the well-oiled machine I felt the US military had become? Some of the oil is leaking out. A few people are starting to say, "I can't get it done." Every time this happens, it has a domino effect. The tanker cancels, so the F-4G cancels, so the B-52 cancels. It really drives home the point that this Air Force thing is a real team effort. A chain can be no stronger than its weakest link.

0555, 21 January. We're sitting in the plane, preparing to go. It feels better to be here than back in the room. Time on my hands really screws up my head. Written on one of our M-117 bombs: "Didn't Qadhafi tell you not to ____ with the USAF?"

0937, 21 January. Homeward bound. We had to abort our primary, heavily defended target due to a Wild Weasel no-show, but we hit a lightly defended secondary target. I'm feeling strange emotions. I actually feel a little disappointed about not charging in to get shot. Just goes to show you, don't trust your emotions.

0055, 22 January. I saw the news yesterday. American POWs were on Baghdad TV. My first sensation was fear. What if that happens to me? But that feeling soon changed to a burning rage the like of which I have never felt before. I paced back and forth, back and forth, like a caged animal. All I could think of was how badly I wanted to climb into my bomber and kill Iraqis by the thousands until they let those guys go. And I knew that if that should happen to me, my 300 roommates would kill Iraqis by the thousands until they let me go. And then I was tired and slept.

I walked along with my tail gunner, Doc Johnson, an individual with whom I find comfort in talking, and whom I would describe with words like down-to-earth, sincere, and dependable. He says, "You know man, the longer this war goes on, the less I feel." His comment hit home. I guess we're starting to suffer from emotional burnout.

1345, 22 January. Bomber briefing room. Quotes on the blackboard: "Eat, sleep, _____ , bomb." "Turn pilot, _____ turn, turn this thing around and get the hell out of here." "That's the heaviest AAA I've ever seen!" (This last comment was attributed to a copilot on his first combat mission.)

0715, 24 January. We finished our fourth combat sortie last night. The crew is rapidly becoming combat seasoned and is starting to integrate with high efficiency. All cylinders operated at peak output last night. Our wingman aborted shortly after takeoff, which meant we should abort also or try to join up with another formation. I elected to press on alone into enemy territory. It turned out to be a correct choice. Because we were not in formation, the pilot team worried less about keeping the formation together and stayed more abreast of the threat situation. We saw an enormous expenditure of enemy AAA and missiles aimed at some poor guys making a low-altitude strike. When the first missile popped out of there, Eric saw it while scanning cross cockpit and started yelling, "Missile launch! Missile launch!" We yelled like that for the first two or three launches. By the tenth launch, our calls had become, "There goes another one." The only real threat we had was a barrage of high-altitude AAA shot at us in the target area. It all blew up below us, and we beat feet for home. Meanwhile, I think some Iraqi artillery gunners had their dinner interrupted.

0942, 25 January. Fifth combat mission today. The Iraqis aren't very good, but it's impossible not to be on edge. There's always that lucky shot. We've dropped so many bombs on these guys that we're starting to run out. We now drop 500-pound MK-82s instead of 750-pound M-117s or cluster bomb units. We all hope this will be over soon.

0752, 26 January. War brings into clear focus the important things in life, especially family and religion. I can honestly say I do not fear for my own life, but rather for the lives of my wife and children if I

193

were killed or captured. Thoughts of my wife having to struggle on alone and my son growing to manhood without a father are disturbing in an extreme sense. I have also come to terms with my faith. This is a firm belief in God. I believe he will not judge me by some prayer I have spoken in a church under the auspices of some religious leader, but rather by my actions—by the courage with which I battle injustice, by the fervor with which I work to better the world. I think that some day I might like to be a teacher.

Speaking of religion, we have moved to a new, far more comfortable dwelling which happens to be located right next to a mosque. We have the dubious pleasure of listening to Islamic prayers five times a day. It is a decidedly unholy sound, and it leaves no doubt in my mind that I am in a strange place far from home.

1912, 28 January. Last night we flew a bombing raid on the most heavily defended target yet struck by B-52s. It was a Scud missile support facility on the Syrian border that had been supplying the launchers for attacks against Israel. Some children were killed in a Scud attack the previous night. We took off as "number two" in a three-ship formation. We lost our gunnery system shortly after takeoff, but we pressed on. The rest of the trip north was uneventful with the exception of several massive AAA expenditures, none of which reached our altitude. Two minutes prior to the bomb run, the electronic warfare officer announced in a despairing voice that we had lost our ALR-20 scope, the primary instrument used to identify and monitor enemy threats and to determine our tactical and electronic countermeasures response.

My mind raced. I would be jeopardizing the aircraft and crew if I pressed on, but I despised the thought of breaking off the attack and withholding the weapons. Further, with no gunnery system or ALR-20 scope, we would be flying home with very little defensive capability. The copilot was frantically gesturing to me to strike the target. We were three minutes away from dropping 30,000 pounds of high explosives on a bunch of baby killers, so on we went through a salvo of enemy missiles, toward the target. One whizzed by our left wing and exploded above the aircraft.

Bombs away, and a couple of minutes later we were out of missile range and heading home while burning liquid rocket propellant lit the night sky over Iraq. Back at the operations building, some tanker guys walked by wearing flak jackets. A grizzly old master sergeant grumbled, "A tanker guy wearing a flak jacket is like a poodle wearing a spiked collar." Tanker drivers are now called "poodles."

1937, 3 February. The last couple of missions were pretty quiet. Nothing came up at us at all while we were striking the bad guys. One of the missions was somewhat gratifying. We were planned as usual against the Republican Guard; but just before takeoff, a truck came up with a message giving us new coordinates. We were now supposed to hit the Kuwaiti/Saudi border about five miles in from the coast. US Marines were dug in about five miles south of our target. Apparently the Iraqis were massing forces there for an incursion into Saudi Arabia.

I felt uncomfortable about dropping 51 bombs from 38,000 feet that close to friendly troops, but we cruised on up there anyway. When the radar navigator flipped the radar on, he said, "You wouldn't believe what my cross hairs fell on. It looks like a city down there." That was on the night of 31 January. The next day we learned that a Marine general had called to say, "Good show!" Marine observers reported trucks flying around, and a British reporter said, "Waves of B-52s had struck the Iraqi armored columns." (There were three of us in the formation.) I understand the price of miniature B-52 models has tripled on the front lines.

The food here is becoming grosser by the day. Yucko! We eat strictly for sustenance. We get no enjoyment out of it. I didn't realize how spoiled I was back in the States. I think more and more about going home to my family and doing something for fun. This war is only 18 days old, but it seems like I've been here forever.

1413, 7 February. Preparing to fly. We are becoming harder and stronger with each passing day. We've become accustomed to the routine, which is really no routine at all. I go out and run every other day and no longer feel tired all of the time. I can usually sleep five or six hours at a stretch now, and I catnap when I can (usually in the plane over friendly territory). Physically, I feel as though I could go on indefinitely. I'll bet Saddam Hussein isn't sleeping too well these days. Words to a song—"An honest man's pillow is his peace of mind."

1402, 12 February. Show time in five and one-half hours. We will pound the Iraqis some more. We hit an oil refinery three nights ago. I understand it's still on fire. Night before last, 12 B-52s hit a military complex just north of Baghdad. I'll bet that woke them up. Too bad we didn't get to go.

I think about going home, making love to my wife, playing with my kids. Back here, hundreds of miles from the front, we have a pretty luxurious existence compared to the Army guys, and we know it. But how much we want to go home is exactly the same.

War is a different experience for a pilot than for a ground troop. We only visit the war. They live it. I prefer my vantage point, thank you. Although we have no access to such information, I feel certain the ground war will commence within a week.

1919, 23 February. OK, so I was wrong. But the president's deadline expires in 20 minutes, so I'll bet something is going to happen soon. Total apathy has set in at this point. The Iraqis only shoot back once in a blue moon. We just climb in the airplane every day, drop our bombs on someone or something, and come back. Little things, or even big things, don't bother us any more. Tonight promises to be a bit different. We're going out on Scud patrol. Going to hang out over Iraq for a few hours and wait until someone sees a launcher or a launch and then go drop on it. Odds are we'll just fly in circles and come back. Eric and I have been toying with the idea of calling up Baghdad

Radio and giving them position reports. Maybe the ground offensive will start tonight and we'll get a light show. This war is getting old.

1933, 25 February. The ground war is in full swing now, with allied forces advancing on Kuwait City. You know, it's funny. People back in the States write and talk about how helpless they feel and how they wish they could do something to help. Tonight as I watched CNN interview the families of ground troops, it was my turn to feel helpless. Bad weather is preventing visual weapon release, and the proximity of friendly troops prohibits our radar deliveries. Consequently, the USAF is unable to bring its tremendous firepower to bear against the Republican Guard. I heard that some close air support is getting in, but we can't really scatter their teeth and eyeballs around the way we would like to. I hope we don't take many casualties. I'll bet the Kuwaiti flag flies over Kuwait City by midday tomorrow.

Where's the Beer?

1623, 3 March. With a cease-fire in effect and the Iraqi Army virtually destroyed, it appears the war is over. We flew 27 missions. On our 26th mission, a surface-to-air missile hit my wingman. Despite numerous system failures and fuel leaks from more than 50 holes, the B-52's system redundancy allowed the crew to bring it home. They said the impact was tremendous, and they were sure she was going to break up. But she didn't! If you're a bomber pilot, you've got to like that. Coincidentally, on this mission, the pilot's ejection seat in our aircraft was inoperative. I decided to accept the aircraft since we hadn't been shot at on the last six missions, and with the ground war in progress, I couldn't stand the thought of holding back the weapons. I imagine the look on my face was priceless when I heard, "I've been hit!!" on the radio.

As for us, these are days of sitting by the pool, doing jigsaw puzzles, and playing cards. Even though no one is shooting at us, and we are living a leisurely life, those same five words keep going around in my head—I want to go home!

1231, 9 March. Walk in the grass, swing on a swing, ice cold beer, and MTV. How much the simple pleasures can come to mean. Coast inbound on the greatest country on the planet earth. I know, I know, we do have our problems. But at least we the people have mechanisms, rusty though they may be, to solve those problems. In a world where the law of the jungle is the rule of the day, this country, my country, to people around the world, serves as an example of the height that civilization can reach. And still, just as it did one hundred years ago, it shines to them in the distance as a beacon of justice and freedom and hope. I hope that in some small way, my efforts and the efforts of my comrades who risked, and in some cases gave, their lives have brightened that beacon and helped to preserve and further American ideals for people around the world for generations to come. God bless the land of the free and the home of the brave!

Killing from the High Ground

by

1st Lt James O. Clonts

I looked around my room for the last time and wondered if I would ever see it again. I deposited my wedding ring and wallet in a drawer with a letter to my wife, turned off the light, and locked the door behind me. As I stepped out into the cool moonlit Indian Ocean night, I took a deep breath of air. The strong smell of sea spray invigorated me. I saw dozens of young men, burdened with flight gear, moving toward several waiting blue buses. I picked up my heavy flight bag, tossed my jacket and helmet bag over one shoulder, my flak jacket over the other, and made my way towards the crowd of young warriors.

The bus ride was quiet, not much laughing or joking. Solemn young men, far from home, watched an alien landscape pass by outside, each man deep in thought. Some had their eyes closed, either praying or sleeping, I couldn't tell. What did fate have in store for us tonight? Would we be walking the shores of this little island 24 hours from now, or would we be lost in a godforsaken desert deep in the heart of a bad-guy land? Or would we be dead?

Up until a few months ago, we lived very constant lives. Bomber crews rarely fly far from home in peacetime. We went from Hometown USA, our nice houses, cars, and loving families to a small British island in the middle of the Indian Ocean. We were as far from home as we could be on this small planet. Now, in the middle of the night, we were going off to kill men we'd never met . . . and they would try to kill us.

The bus pulled up in front of Base Operations, and we piled off. We swamped into life support and picked up our helmets, survival vests, chemical warfare gear, and bulletproof vests. Once we had loaded the bus, we made our way to the main briefing room. In the hall just before the large, ominous double doors, a lone airman was setting up a food table for our preflight meal . . . or last supper. I peeked under the lid and saw steak and fries! I thought about our boys up on the front line, eating sand for dinner while they waited for the ground war to start. My moment of pity lasted for about three seconds because our war had already started.

Once inside the briefing room, we read our seating order and position in tonight's strike package. We were going to lead a three-ship of B-52s. We took our places in the front row and waited for the staff to bring us our mission. The tension was still thick, and many of us had bags under our eyes from tossing and turning all night.

I looked down the row at my crew. It took six men to fly a B-52. The aircraft commander and copilot flew the jet, the radar navigator and navigator directed the plane and dropped the bombs, and the electronic warfare officer and gunner defended the plane by jamming radars and shooting down enemy fighters. We worked together as a crew. If we did our jobs right, we would destroy our target and return alive.

I was the navigator, fresh out of school with almost as many combat hours as training hours. I was scared, to say the least—we all were. The beauty of fighting as a crew is the strength of numbers. We were all scared, but together we were greater than the sum of our parts. A feeling of shared risk, of trusting each other with our lives, of camaraderie and loyalty pulled us together to conquer any individual fears. We were a killing machine about to go into action.

The briefers finally brought us the mission. The room was secured for secret information. It was right out of some WWII movie: "Gentlemen, your target for tonight is . . . ."

That night we were to strike a Republican Guard artillery position. The target was inside Iraq . . . deep inside Iraq. We would spend about 40 minutes in enemy territory.

The targeteers gave us our target study. Intelligence briefed the threats: enemy fighters, antiaircraft artillery, and surface-to-air missiles. We received a weather briefing and a chaplain's blessing. The wing commander gave us his usual pep talk. When these briefings were finished, it was time to throw down some chow and fill water bottles. Once that mission was complete, the bus took us out to the plane.

Clonts, Kennedy, Holland, McHugh, and Simon

In the midnight light, I saw dozens of dark, ominous shapes on the vast flight line. Some of these shapes were KC-135s and KC-10s. The rest of those shapes carried more potent payloads than jet fuel. The big, gray bombers, wings drooping under the weight of fuel and bombs, sat waiting, ready for flight.

Each 1950s-vintage plane carried eight turbojet engines, 280,000 pounds of jet fuel, and 37,000 pounds of M-117s (750-pound iron bombs). Tonight they would also carry my friends and me. Men on the ground would try to destroy these harbingers of death and the men inside them. If they succeeded, we would die. If they failed, they would die.

The bus stopped in front of one plane with a grinding of brakes and a slight squeal. We unloaded our gear and stood by while the pilot read the forms, the recent history of this plane. I gazed at the big bomber with awe, from the sensors in the nose, past the drooping wings, back to the four .50-caliber machine guns in the tail. My gaze

201

stopped on a set of numbers on the tail: 57-6473. This plane had been built in 1957, nine years before I was born.

With the forms in order, we began the preflight. I went up into the belly of the beast, the downstairs navigators' compartment. We sat behind and below the pilots, our only windows were monitors linked to cameras in the nose. I completed my checklist and went outside to help preflight the bombs.

We carried 45 M-117s and each had to be checked, a time-consuming task. We checked linkages and fuse settings, and we pulled all of the safety pins.

While we worked on our lethal payload, the pilots completed their walk-around inspection. The gunner was checking his guns and the electronic warfare (EW) officer was checking his antennas and transmitters. He also had a full load of chaff (radar reflecting foil) and flares (chunks of magnesium that burn very hot to decoy missiles) to check.

Once we convinced ourselves that all was in order, the pilots started engines. I turned on the offensive avionics system, the navigation and bombing computer. It would take about 50 minutes to align the inertial navigation units properly. These special gyros sense changes in acceleration and, when linked to a computer, can calculate our position in space.

Finally, the three big bombers began to taxi. We took off in one-minute intervals, then joined up and flew in two-mile intervals stacked 500 feet apart vertically. We led, so the other two spaced off us. We used the radar to determine spacing.

My first job as navigator was to meet the tanker on time at the air refueling rendezvous point (without using the radio). Timing was critical, and the other two would simply follow my lead.

Finally the two KC-135s came into view. We moved into position, and the tanker lowered its air refueling boom down to us. The pilot held us in position while the boom operator on the tanker plugged into us. We took on 60,000 pounds of fuel and moved away so the number three bomber could get half his gas. He got the other half from the other tanker when the number two bomber finished.

After air refueling, we continued north toward a waiting war. About an hour and a half later, we completed our second air refueling.

This topped off our tanks for the journey across Saudi Arabia, into Iraq, and back out.

We coasted in over Saudi Arabia approximately five hours after takeoff. Following two more hours of cruise over Saudi Arabia, we'd be in the thick of it. The EW passed out our standard issue .38-caliber Smith & Wessons and 18 rounds of ammunition. We knew if we ever needed to use the pistol, there would be no chance to reload.

One by one the crew began donning bulletproof vests and shoulder holsters. We strapped on survival knives and stuffed every pocket with maps, water, and survival gear. If we had to bail out, I don't think I could have run away, as burdened as I was.

At this point, I adjusted timing so that we released our weapons on time. Each bomb produces a blast fragmentation pattern several thousand feet high. Any aircraft flying through this would certainly be damaged, possibly downed. We don't drop just one bomb, we drop up to 51 bombs in a train half a mile long and a thousand feet wide. Three bombers will lay down up to 153 bombs in an area a few miles square. In other words, the sky opens up and death descends upon the earth. If you are not directly hit by the shrapnel, the shock wave can deafen you and cause nose and ear bleeding. Some call it carpet bombing, but that is not very accurate. The radar navigator can put a bomb within killing distance of a tank. But the middle bomb dropped is the one that hits the target. It will leave 22 bombs in front of the target and 22 bombs behind. This allows for his aiming to be a little long or short. The bomb train "steps" across the target.

I accelerated, and we configured the aircraft weapons for release. About 30 minutes from the border, we heard via satellite that our target had changed. (The B-52 has global communication capability through satellites.) Our EW and gunner quickly decoded the message and passed the new coordinates to us. We plotted them and found the target had moved about a mile. We confirmed the target with the other bombers on a secure voice radio.

We were close to the border, so the pilots turned off the exterior lights. We checked in with our airborne warning and control system (AWACS) plane, "Rambo Flight, checking in as fragged." They replied that our target area picture was "clear," meaning there were no threats in the area. The EW reported some friendly fighters on his scope. That was reassuring.

Almost immediately after I told the crew we were crossing the border, the EW said he had a missile threat on his scope. After several seconds, the missile threat went down and we continued. Every few minutes or so, he would announce a new threat, and we'd hold our breath until the missile radar shut down. AWACS still called the picture "clear."

We pressed on to the target area when AWACS called us with a threat. A flight of F-4G Wild Weasels spotted two missile launches along our route of flight. We plotted the coordinates. The missile sight was just 40 miles off the nose. We quickly turned the cell 30 degrees right and accelerated. Once we were abeam the missile sight, we turned back to the target.

On the bomb run, we could see antiaircraft artillery (AAA) being fired at us. It tracked us across the sky. The AAA couldn't reach us at our altitude, but they sure tried. We were on time for release, and I double-checked the switches and release settings. The radar navigator and I completed our checklists, and he began aiming the bombs. His radar scope was configured to focus on the target area. He moved his cross hairs onto the largest blip, the artillery position. After cross-checking his aiming, I examined the radar cross hairs, and I saw several large vehicles or tanks arranged in a triangle with a bright blob in the middle. I reasoned this must be what an artillery position looks like at night from 38,000 feet.

I counted down the seconds to release and, at zero, called, "Bombs away!" To my left I could see the bomb indicator lights going out as each bomb fell into space. After three seconds, they were all out. It would be another 50 seconds until the first bomb hit the ground. I thought about the enemy artillery position down below and the men in it. They didn't know they had 50 seconds to live. There was no stopping the bombs, no place to hide, not even an indication they were under the cross hairs on my radar scope seconds before. I started a stopwatch at bombs away, and I couldn't help but watch as it counted down the last seconds of those men's lives. They were Saddam's men, maybe not willingly, but they kept him in power all the same.

They may be his pawns, but they're also the tool he used to conquer and destroy. I pitied their lives, but I would not spare them.

As the watch showed 50 seconds, there was a reassuring flash of light on my TV screen. I felt many mixed emotions, the strongest of which was satisfaction. They'd failed tonight—I was alive.

We didn't see any more threats that night. We left enemy airspace and rendezvoused with a KC-135 for our last refueling. After topping off, we coasted back home and landed on Diego Garcia 16 hours after takeoff.

On the way home, I had time to reflect on life, death, war, and peace. I wondered how many men we'd killed. I was incensed that Saddam could bring this terrible "storm" on his people. The truth of the matter is that we Americans are better killers than Iraqis. They kill more often and maybe like it better than us, but when forced to kill, there is just no one better at the art of war.

We kill through cunning, stealth, technology, strategy, and intestinal fortitude. We don't like to kill. I didn't like to kill, but the blood on my hands doesn't bother me. The world knows America doesn't want war, but when forced into it, we know no equal.

Maybe it is the value we place on human life. We cherish each human life so much that when we are forced to kill, we take it more seriously. Looking back at the war, I realize that I didn't hate the enemy and I didn't pity the enemy. I simply killed the enemy.

Tactical Airlift Operations

by

1st Lt Neal A. Thagard

At 2330 on 14 August 1990, the silence of the night was broken by the telephone's ring. I scrambled to answer, and I heard the impersonal voice of the squadron duty officer (DO) on the other end. Our conversation was clipped and staccato.

DO: Pack for an indefinite period of TDY!

Me: How long is that?

DO: I don't know.

Me: Where am I going?

DO: Can't tell you.

Me: Somewhere in the Middle East?

DO: That's a good guess.

Me: How long do I have to pack?

DO: One hour.

In a blur, I packed, tried to tell my wife and son that I didn't know where I was going or for how long, and told them good-bye. It was a frightening good-bye. It had the bite of a last good-bye.

We loaded our C-130E Hercules and, on departure, still didn't know our ultimate destination. By dawn, we were over the Atlantic and headed for Abu Dhabi, United Arab Emirates (UAE). By 16 August, we were in what would be our home for the next eight months.

After the initial fury of crossing half the globe and settling in an alien land, things calmed down. The flying schedule was full. We were carrying troops and equipment all over the Arabian Peninsula. Of course, after a while, it became somewhat routine. At this point, the burning question was, "When are we going home?" For months that was the theme of our lives. On 17 January 1991, all of this changed.

At 3:30 A.M. our emergency sirens began blaring. The PA system announced, "All personnel, this is not an exercise. Go MOPP Level 4 (Mission-oriented Protective Posture; i.e., chemical gear). Repeat. This is not an exercise. Go MOPP Level 4. Check your neighbors. Repeat. Check your neighbors."

Moments later, another officer came in, yelling "Jesus Christ, it's happening. We've been bombing Kuwait City and Baghdad. Wave after wave of B-52s are slamming the Iraqis. The F-16s are taking out Kuwait City. I can't believe it."

It was like something you had waited for forever, wanting it to happen, but not wanting it to happen. Half of you wanted to get on with it while the other half never wanted to see it begin. Not if it meant human lives. But here it was. The deadline was past. Now it was war.

The next day, every plane in the squadron was airborne. In full combat regalia, we started pushing west. We began an intense redeployment of the 101st Airborne to Rafhā Air Base, Saudi Arabia, 18 miles from the Iraqi border. I saw the faces of the soldiers in our cargo bay. Young faces of men who weren't old enough to buy a drink, staring back in puzzlement over where we were headed. One private asked me where we were taking them. I pointed to the spot on the chart. I saw the apprehension in his eyes, along with a look of knowing. We both knew this was war and everything that comes with it. Veterans from other wars always tell you that combat is frightening. It's the most devastating fear. But, somehow, you think it will be different for you. As the private and I perused the chart, we both shared that unspoken fear that all men in war come to know. Moments later, we popped the hatch. He was out the door, in the sand, headed north.

For days, our routine was unchanging. We'd fuel up, pick up men and equipment from Dhahran Air Base, Saudi Arabia, and head for the border. Day and night blurred together. Living in a chemical suit became second nature. The line of men waiting to be carried north appeared endless. Our C-130s set up a caravan, flying into sand landing strips that were too small for bigger aircraft. Some of us even landed on sections of highway, even closer to the border.

208

Many other things had become routine at this point, including Scud attacks on Dhahran and Riyadh. The assaults on Dhahran became so common that no one wanted to land in "Scud City" after sunset. We went in because we had to, but we always knew where the nearest bomb shelter was.

The C-130 is an old, venerable, and reliable aircraft, but it's defenseless. It's only true defense against antiaircraft artillery (AAA) and surface-to-air missiles (SAM) is to avoid being seen. We fly low to do that, 300 feet above ground level (AGL). But even at 300 feet AGL, a 100-foot-long aircraft paints a huge silhouette. Often, the desert environment wouldn't allow us to fly that low. So each mission carried with it the possibility of crossing the path of a SAM.

Finally, our most rewarding missions began: taking US Army troops out of Iraq to begin their journey home. Our first flight was into Jalibah Air Base, Iraq. The runway was 10,000 feet long, but we had only 4,500 feet available (due to bomb craters in the center of the airstrip). During most of our flight, we had no visibility because the smoke from bombings and oil fires was impenetrable. At 10,000 feet altitude, it was literally as dark as night. Our only means of finding and identifying the airfield was by picking it out on radar. We call this an airborne radar approach (ARA). Basically, I had to find the airfield and talk the pilot down to a safe approach altitude. Our first pass went smoothly. We touched down and picked up our passengers. However, our second and final approach was not so smooth.

The layer of smoke (from oil fires) stopped at about 500 feet AGL. The problem was a raging sand storm below the smoke layer. Our visibility was less than 100 feet. I guess just knowing that these men had been in the sand, without a shower or decent food for over 3 months, drove us to attempt a hazardous approach. We were within one mile (30 seconds) of the field, but we still couldn't see the runway. As we closed the gap, we began a slow descent. We never saw the field until we were literally on top of it. The pilot decided to try to land anyway. He maneuvered aggressively, but we ended up in a stall. I saw him pulling back on the yoke with all his strength, trying to get her to climb. The tendons on the back of his neck, tanned from months in the desert sun, were taut with exertion. His forearms bore

209

the same stress. The ground moved up closer to meet us. I could see individual blades of grass on the ground. As time slowed, I thought I may never see my wife or son again. It would have been so unfair to live through the war, only to die now. But then, a half-second later, we began ascending.

I talked to some of the men we pulled out of the sand. The company we were carrying had seven casualties. Two were from combat, five were from souvenir hunting. The irony of those deaths is the most painful, to live through the war and die from tripping booby traps while picking up a war memento. One soldier pulled an Iraqi helmet from an enemy bunker. His right arm and leg were blown off.

I'm home now. My squadron had the standard "grand" return, complete with a band, politicians, and the press. Months later, I ask myself if I'm any different. Sure! No one's ever the same. But I figured my family was the same—until the failed coup in the Soviet Union. Hours before dawn, I was pulling on my flight suit for a local training flight. I mentioned to my drowsy wife that a coup had occurred overnight in Russia. My wife sat bolt upright. "How does that affect you?", she asked. No, I guess my family isn't the same.

One Long Night

by

Capt Timothy D. Broeking

On the evening of 27 February 1991, my crew and I were alerted from Bravo standby to be part of an eight-ship formation that would conduct a resupply drop for the 101st Airborne Division. We would lead the third element of the formation.

Intelligence briefed the general situation for the area we were dropping in, and we began planning the mission. Severe rain and lightning delayed the loading, so the mission commander broke the formation into three individual elements. These elements would launch as they completed loading. Suddenly, my crew was the element lead for the last two aircraft. We spent the extra time afforded us by the slow loading schedule to preflight night vision goggles (NVG) for the copilot and the second navigator. We also talked about the self-contained navigation system (SCNS) that we were about to use for only the second time since arriving.

We finally took off at 0140, 28 February 1991, four hours after scheduled and a little over an hour after the second formation had departed. Immediately after takeoff, we were in the weather, dodging thunderstorms around the airfield at King Fahd. Once we escaped the weather, we found ourselves about 10 minutes late. That ordinarily wouldn't have been a big deal for a three-hour ingress, but we had a specific corridor to fly and airspeed to hold. That didn't give us much leeway. After talking with the pilot, we decided to speed up and risk running over someone ahead of us. We figured the only aircraft ahead of us were our second formation, and no matter how fast we flew, we wouldn't catch them. We were right, and we didn't see anyone but the first formation coming back from their drops.

211

Ready to Go

As we neared the front lines, we turned off all exterior lights except for our top formation lights, and we descended to 500 feet above the ground for crossing the border. It was pitch black outside, and neither the second navigator nor the copilot could see much with their NVGs. I shut the radar down to avoid being detected by Iraqi air defenses. We flew the SCNS system backed up by old-fashioned ground-speed-and-timing dead reckoning. The SCNS brought us to the initial point (IP), an Iraqi airfield that had been captured by the 101st sometime earlier in the ground war. We didn't pick it out until we were turning overhead with the NVGs, but we managed to identify it.

Our gamble with airspeed paid off, and we were 30 seconds ahead as we turned at the IP for our 60-mile run into the drop zone. This was to our advantage because the winds were not what we had expected. We rolled out into over 60 knots of headwind. We kept losing time even after pushing the throttles to our wingman's maximum indicated airspeed. We contacted the airborne battlefield command and control center (ABCCC) in the area with our inbound call. They

212

told us we were still a "go," and they wanted to confirm drop-zone coordinates. Unfortunately, the coordinates they gave us plotted out 30 miles east of the briefed coordinates. After some discussion, the crew decided to go to the briefed coordinates. We knew the first and second formations had dropped there and had received confirmation of good drops from the ground party. We figured if there wasn't anyone at the first drop zone, we would go to the second and drop there.

Our luck stayed with us. Just before the one minute warning, the ground party radioed they could hear us. We proceeded in, but we aborted the first drop because we couldn't spot the three lights that had been briefed as the point of impact. After racetracking back out, the ground party asked us to flash a light so they could help us find them. We weren't thrilled about that idea, but we flashed a retracted landing light so we could drop the load. The light worked, and we lined up with the ground party's single remaining light (the other two had burned out earlier). The second navigator and the wingman dropped with the NVGs. The ground party confirmed a good drop, and we headed home into an already lightening sky.

We landed at 0619, and we were greeted with the news that a cease-fire would start at 0800. We were all tired, but we were very happy to have done the only night combat drop in the theater, as far as we knew. And we were happy that the war was over. We found out during the debrief that the ABCCC had given the wrong coordinates. Also an Iraqi MiG-25 had been flying in our area, and the flashes we had seen approximately 30 miles from the drop zone were from a mortar battle on the Euphrates River.

This mission epitomized the type of crew coordination tactical airlift missions require. While we don't get much glory, we do get a lot of satisfaction from overcoming obstacles and completing the mission.

Babb, Krzysik, Broeking, Dever, and Alvarado

C-141 Operations

by

Capt Eric D. Haussermann

My most enduring memory of Desert Shield/Desert Storm is fatigue. From the first mission into Saudi Arabia in mid-August to the routine ammunition run in February, the one constant a C-141B pilot could look forward to was exhaustion.

The ordeal of the first few days of Desert Shield was an indication of what the next year would be like for a strategic airlift pilot. I remember watching television broadcast the news that Iraq had invaded Kuwait. Since my job description was wrapped around the motto, "You call, we haul," I figured I would be leaving soon.

It was no surprise when every crew member at Norton AFB, regardless of rank or staff position, was put on Bravo alert the following day. Bravo alert means pack your bags and sleep, because you may be launched in 12 hours. Everyone knew we were going to the Middle East. About eight o'clock that evening, the call came to report to base.

The squadron room was very crowded. Everyone was briefed en masse while picking up mission orders and finding crew assignments. Once I assembled my crew, we threw our bags on a bus with about five other crews and headed over to pick up our chemical warfare suits. The mood was serious.

After picking up the chemical gear and arming ourselves with the standard .38-caliber revolver, we ended up in a processing center in the base operations building. Long lines formed for flak jackets and gamma globulin shots; I wouldn't sit down properly for a few hours. We were then bused out to the waiting aircraft.

I was with one of 18 crews heading to Rhein Main AB, Germany, to start the flow of men and materiel into the Desert Shield area of responsibility (AOR). We stopped at Pope AFB; after all, somebody had to pick up the 82d Airborne and take them to Saudi Arabia. Then we flew to Germany and the disorganized mess that we called "the Frankfurt stage."

All "duty day" and "crew rest" rules had been discarded. The Rhein Main command post told my crew we had 10 hours to eat and sleep, then we had to be ready to go. They gave us no idea of what to expect. They found a room to pack us into, and after about six hours of often-interrupted sleep, we were up, bags packed, ready to go. Surprise! Command post had no information for my crew. About 10 hours after waking up, everyone was ready to go back to bed, but then we were alerted. Our destination, eastern Saudi Arabia.

Unfamiliar routes, flight plans, radio procedures, and airfields are often encountered by Military Airlift Command C-141 crews. During that first eight-hour leg to Dhahran, we became part of an air bridge from the United States to the Middle East that became very familiar in the coming months. But it was new that first night. From Europe to Saudi Arabia, the night sky was filled with heavies, all heading east. Every few miles, there was a C-141, C-5, or contract flight, all using the MAC call sign, all part of the same team.

At this early stage of Desert Shield, there was no flow control. When we arrived at Dhahran, we were one of about 30 strategic airlifters trying to find a place to park. We finally squeezed into a corner of the ramp and pushed our cargo off the airplane. The servicing folks weren't ready for us. They had only three or four gas trucks available at the time, and we were told to expect a couple of hours' wait for fuel. Eight hours later, we finally had our gas and took off for Germany.

After another eight-hour trip back to Frankfurt, we were feeling the effects of our 30-hour day. Command post gave us another 10 hours to eat and sleep, then we were off to the desert once again. That was the last time I felt fully rested for more than a year.

Things weren't any easier in the following months, but I became accustomed to the routine. During a typical mission, we took off from home station in the United States, picked up cargo somewhere in the country, and flew to Charleston AFB or McGuire AFB, the US staging bases. After sleeping and eating, we flew to Upper Heyford or Mildenhall in Britain, Torrejon or Zaragoza in Spain, or Frankfurt in Germany. From the European staging bases, we flew shuttles into the AOR for about two weeks, then we flew back to Norton.

I usually had from one to five days at home, enough time to pay bills, wash laundry, and sleep. Then I took off and did it all over again. This simple routine continued through Desert Storm. I encountered plenty of screwups and dangers from day to day, but at least they relieved the boredom.

Some of the more typical problems I encountered included the many times I was alerted to an empty aircraft. (Convincing command post to find some cargo to fly down to the AOR was a hassle.) Frequently, we were told to take our cargo to one destination and, after arriving at the aircraft, my loadmaster would tell me the cargo had been tagged for another destination.

Some incidents were more frustrating. We waited for takeoff almost two hours at the end of Torrejon's runway while the apathetic traffic controllers held us for arriving traffic at Baharas International. It made me wonder whether the Spanish were backing the war effort.

Some difficulties were dangerous. Whenever we flew into Riyadh at night while the city was under Scud attack, I always hoped the Patriot missiles didn't mistake a C-141 for a Scud! Our greatest danger was our own tired people.

Back-to-back 24-to-30-hour duty days, combined with multiple time zone crossings and constant disruptions in circadian rhythms, took its toll on airlift crews. I was personally involved in two incidents in which fatigue nearly caused fatal accidents. During one long flight from Saudi Arabia to Spain, the controllers changed my route. As the copilot and I were looking at our charts to determine where we were going, the autopilot disengaged—and neither of us noticed. I felt something was wrong, however, and I looked up to discover my plane had entered a 70-degree left bank and 40-degree nose-low attitude. I safely recovered the aircraft, but I don't particularly enjoy unusual attitude recoveries outside the simulator.

An even more exciting event occurred when we were arriving back at Torrejon after a 28-hour day. I was the third pilot, and I was sitting

217

in the jump seat for the approach and landing. The aircraft commander was new and in the left seat while the copilot was flying the aircraft from the right seat. We were all dead tired. Quite a few radio calls had to be repeated to us on approach, and the copilot kept forgetting what altitudes to level off at on the way down. These were bad signs. During the tight visual approach to runway 5, I could tell early in the final turn we were overshooting the runway to the left. I suggested a go-around. No one acknowledged. The copilot put in a large correction, causing the aircraft to overshoot to the right, putting us between the runway and the taxiway, 20 feet off the ground. The aircraft commander still hadn't said a word. By this point, I was screaming, "GO AROUND!!" The copilot dipped the left wing, thought better of it, and commenced a missed approach. A friend of mine, in a taxiing aircraft, told me our left wing came within one foot of the ground. Fatigue almost got us.

Fortunately, we won the war; and by August 1991, I had finally caught up on my sleep. Flying strategic aircraft during Desert Shield/ Desert Storm was demanding but rewarding. I may have a few extra wrinkles and some more grey hairs, but I wouldn't have missed that show for anything—not even an extra hour or two of sleep!

Desert Journal

by

Capt Edward Fisher

When I deployed to Shaikh Isa AB, Bahrain, for Desert Storm, I kept a journal in which I made daily entries. Here are excerpts of my entries.

30 January 1991 (Wednesday), 1900 hours local time, Shaikh Isa AB, Bahrain.

I finally arrived in the war zone today! For the first week and a half of the war, I had watched from Clark AB, Philippines, chomping at the bit. I was one of six standby volunteer crews (12 men) ready for deployment, yet there I sat. Then we got the word we were going.

Of course the flight was delayed. We finally left on Monday, 28 January, for what we thought would be a quick flight with a couple of stops. But the crew of the chartered Hawaiian Airlines DC-8 needed rest, so we stopped for "17 hours" in Diego Garcia. Since the next base was too crowded to grant us landing privileges, this stop became one-and-a-half days of lollygagging around on the beach. Some B-52 crews stationed there heard we were Wild Weasels and bought us all we could drink. It appears that Weasels are well liked in this war. We finally left early this morning and pulled into Bahrain International late in the morning. One hour-long bus ride later, we were here, having passed a couple of camels on the way.

Everybody carries a pistol and a gas mask all the time. The atmosphere is very relaxed, though. All the crews have been flying hard, and they are telling war stories. It looks like I won't fly until three or four days from now, probably Saturday. We have to in-process first.

2 February 1991 (Saturday), 2340 hours (after first flight).

Tonight, I flew my first combat mission. We were part of Coors 71 flight (all Weasel missions are named after brands of beer). We took off at 1905 on a 2.9-hour mission to support three B-52s and four Saudi Tornados on strikes against the Republican Guard. About 10 miles south of the target, the antiaircraft artillery fire started getting close. It was at our altitude, about 25,000 to 30,000 feet. We said, "The hell with this!" and turned the jet away. No use flying straight into the bullets! We worked around the area of the heaviest fire. We saw a lot of lighter flak at about 15,000 feet and, intermittently, some more heavy stuff came up with us. I picked up several radar signals on my electronic gear, but I was unable to get enough information to shoot them. The signals went on and off the air (up and down in our terminology), but they stayed mostly off.

In the Arming Area, Ready for Takeoff

Capts Ed Fisher and Vinnie Farrell

We wandered through southern Iraq and northern Kuwait, hoping to bait somebody, but we had no luck. But good for the Saudis: We saw secondary explosions and a large fire in the target area during their time over target (TOT). All in all, the adrenaline pumped, and we (Vinnie and I) did pretty good for a couple of "cherry boys." We go back for more of the same tomorrow night.

15 February 1991 (Friday), 1030 hours (after tenth mission).

Last night as part of Coors 65 Flight, I sent a valentine to Saddam—an AGM-88 high-speed anti-radiation missile (HARM). We were the second of two four ships of Weasels. We supported the second half of 12 B-52s striking Ish Kandar, south of Baghdad. There were also EF-111s and F-15s.

221

On the way up, we saw the usual fires and explosions off in the distance in Kuwait. Vinnie was giving me astronomy lessons, pointing out the various constellations.

As we entered the target area, all was quiet. As the BUFFs started hitting their targets, the triple-A came up. I had been working an SA-2, but I had little information. It was within 10 nautical miles of the target. Suddenly, a B-52 called out he had an SA-2 missile, guidance up. I didn't, but nonetheless I acted almost instinctively. I called for Vinnie to select the HARM, but we got a failure on that missile. We selected the other HARM, and "Magnum," we shot at the SA-2. The signal was dotted (not emitting radar energy) and a long way off. There was a two-minute-plus time-of-flight to the target. At about the right time, the signal came back up. At the end of the time-of-flight, the signal went down and stayed down for the rest of the sortie. I was going to call this a probable kill, but my CONRAC recorder did not record the video from my 47, so I couldn't verify impact time versus signal activity for sure. I felt as though we had done a hot job, and no aircraft were lost. That was the bottom line.

The BUFFs hit something last night. We saw many fires and secondary explosions on the ground. It's about time they hit a target. We took off at 2020, landed at 0035, for a 4.3-hour flight.

I have today and tonight off. They're juggling the flight composition. We were in the following order:

1 - Maj Mick "Unable" Elam/Capt Darryl "Rock" Sherman

2 - Capt Dennis "Malf" Malfer/Capt Joe "Pfliegbo" Pflieger

3 - Capt Bob "Dufus" Dupuis/Capt Paul "Data" Dowden

4 - Capt Vince "Vinnie" Farrell/Capt Ed "Tuna" Fisher

The other four of us have been flying as a two-ship elsewhere in the schedule:

1 - Maj Mike "Griff" or "PM" Griffin/Maj William "Sluggo" Sligar

2 - Capt Phil "Spot" Taber/Capt Gene "Geno" Peterson

Now the two-ship is swapping out for 3 and 4, and we'll probably fly as a two-ship for a while.

Capts Bob Dupuis and Ed Fisher

Since the other night when Paul "Data" Dowden worked too far from the target area, Vinnie has taken to calling him "Sir Data" as a joke. Vinnie is quite the cut-up. This nickname comes from the movie *Monty Python and the Holy Grail* and the song about "Brave, brave Sir Robin, who bravely ran away." Vinnie constantly sings this song every flight. I'll probably have nightmares about it for years. Paul is no slouch, but sometimes he is a little over-conservative.

Vinnie and I tend to think we've found the middle ground (all fighter jocks think they have the right solution). We try to work outside or at the edge of the envelope for the threats we've actually seen, and we give consideration to those threats we haven't seen but Intel keeps briefing might be there. But at the same time, there are some risks inherent in our job, and we must never forget we have a mission to perform. If that means overflying an inactive, never seen,

SAM site to work closer to the target, then so be it. We'll make an orbit or two to test the area, then move in. We keep the AAA off to the side, several miles distant. Data and I both agree on that consideration, and Vinnie has gone that route ever since the high-altitude AAA of the first mission gave us a small scare.

1400 Hours

I forgot one thing that happened last night. On the way to the poststrike tanker, we made radio contact. After the preliminaries, someone asked if Malf was in the flight. We said, "Yes." Next, a female voice came over the radio, "Happy Valentine's Day, honey!" Malf's wife was the navigator on the lead tanker. Malf, somewhat embarrassed, gruffly acknowledged his wife's salutation. (Note: We found out days later that this made the news back in the States.)

Capt Vinnie Farrell and His Date

Capts Farrell and Fisher in Native Garb

The First Day

by

Capt Michael S. O'Grady

0400: 17 January 1991

The flight briefing began with the squadron commander saying, "This is it, boys." All thoughts of family or anything else left my mind. My thoughts were on doing the job. This was the first combat mission our squadron would fly in Operation Desert Storm—a 42-ship package of F-16s loaded with two 2,000-pound high-explosive bombs.

We were flying a fairly complicated mission against a Republican Guard command and control center. The mission encompassed four aerial refuelings, including one during darkness. The 42 F-16s would join with a support package of eight F-15s, four F-4Gs, and two EF-111s prior to reaching the Iraqi border.

Finally, the squadron commander said, "Good hunting!" Not a word was spoken, but a feeling of confidence filled the room. I knew this was going to be a tough mission with a lot of threats. I had spent the past eight years training and preparing for this situation, and I knew I was ready! The squadron fully expected to take losses, but somehow my mind accepted that and focused on the task at hand.

As we checked our flight gear, the normal sounds of laughter and conversation were not heard . . . only the clicking of the pilots loading their guns and strapping on their gear. I shook the hands of my flight members and wished them good luck, then I walked to my jet in the dark. The air seemed so peaceful. It was hard to believe that in a few hours these calm skies would be raining destruction.

227

I greeted my crew chief with a salute. He said, "Sir, your jet is ready." I quickly checked the aircraft exterior. I stopped only briefly to write a note to Saddam on the sides of each 2,000-pound bomb strapped under the wings of my fighting machine. Before closing the canopy, my crew chief winked and said, "Sir, see you when you get back."

The formation taxied into position. It was an awesome sight . . . 42 F-16s side by side. The feeling of pride was overwhelming. It was hard to believe that this was the real thing. The sound of the first F-16 rolling down the runway with afterburner cooking jolted my thoughts back to the job at hand.

The flight was picture perfect. The refuelings went as planned, and we rendezvoused with the support package on time. As we crossed the Iraqi border, I thought to myself, "Get ready, the fireworks are about to start." Forty miles from the target, I heard my wingman call out the first of several surface-to-air missiles (SAM) shot at our formation. For the next five minutes, the string of F-16s reacted to an extremely dense network of SAM and antiaircraft fire. This was, no doubt, the longest five minutes of my life.

I rolled in on the target, released the 4,000 pounds of high-explosive bombs on my aim point, then watched my wingman do the same. As we egressed, I looked back. The target area was burning and there were several secondary explosions.

After crossing the border, I felt a sense of euphoria, accomplishment, and relief. As I coasted back to home base, I felt very proud of myself and my squadron. First day, first combat mission, shack (direct hit)! I couldn't wait to congratulate everyone for a job well done. We returned to find the rest of the squadron waiting for our return. The backslapping camaraderie was something I will never forget.

The first day of Operation Desert Storm was a success.

A View from the Cockpit

by

Capt Jack Thompson

This is the story of my most unforgettable mission as an F-16 pilot during Desert Storm. On 19 January 1991, our objective was to destroy a nuclear research facility south of Baghdad. The strike package consisted of 36 F-16s, each carrying two Mk-84 2,000-pound bombs. At that time I was part of the 69th Tactical Fighter Squadron from Moody AFB. We had deployed two weeks earlier and were assigned to a provisional wing already established by Hill AFB. We were equipped with low-altitude navigation and targeting infrared for night (LANTIRN) systems, which allowed us to fight at night. That is how we were primarily used. I flew the first night of the war on 17 January 1991. I didn't fly the next day, so I took advantage of a chance to sleep.

My second combat sortie was my first daytime sortie. The afternoon time over target (TOT) denied us the added security of night flying. I will describe this mission from takeoff through air refueling, ingress, and egress, to return to base (RTB).

Takeoff and air refueling procedures made it difficult to fly the prebriefed formation. Anytime we carry live ordnance, we are restricted by TACR 55-116 to a minimum of 20-second spacing between aircraft. This translates to over 11 minutes (approximately 60–80 miles) between the first and last aircraft of the strike package. Luckily, we were far enough from the forward edge of the battle area (FEBA) for everyone to catch up and build the fighting formation.

If we had been closer to the FEBA, we would not have had time to regroup, especially if we were late taking off and didn't have time to orbit. I was back in the pack, number 31 of 36 aircraft. Eventually I rejoined my flight, and we headed for the tankers. Refueling also made staying in formation difficult. Although we were one big package, we were broken down into flights of four. Each flight had a specific TOT and a certain point in the target area where we were expected to bomb. Since I was number three of my four-ship formation, I was responsible for backing up my flight lead in his responsibilities of navigation and timing, radar search, and returning the flight home safely.

There were five tankers in formation as we rejoined to receive our fuel. Eight F-16s rejoined on each tanker except the last one, which only had four fighters. The tankers were responsible for dropping us off at the Kuwaiti border on time. We would then dash to Baghdad. Timing was crucial on this mission to avoid conflicts between our strike package and others. We all refueled several times, because we wanted as much fuel as possible for the trip "downtown." I knew that fuel was crucial on this mission; every ounce would count. We were in and out of the clouds during refueling, making a demanding task even more complicated.

Finally, our flight finished refueling and we climbed 1,000 to 2,000 feet above the tankers to be in clear weather. We could no longer see the rest of the strike package or the tankers, relying on timing to make our jump on the planned route. We were a few minutes early, so we orbited so as to start the route on time. The altitude, and the combination of heavy fuel loads and bombs, made the airplanes sluggish and unresponsive. My flight lead and his wingman flew out in front of my element by about six miles. I kept asking lead to slow down so I could return to formation, but he didn't respond. I didn't feel comfortable flying over enemy territory out of the briefed formation, so I selected minimum afterburner to close the gap. Unfortunately, I was burning fuel I could't afford to use. I returned to position over Kuwait, but with 1,000 pounds less fuel than I had planned for at this point on the route. I wasn't about to turn back. I started thinking of ways I could return home from the target with enough fuel to meet the tankers waiting for us on the egress. We headed for Baghdad with our fangs out.

Our ingress to the target was uneventful except for a 40-mile radius around Baghdad. AWACS hadn't called out any air threats. With

F-15s escorting our strike package, the Iraqi Air Force probably thought it was best that they didn't come out to play. F-4G Wild Weasels joined our package, ready to slam any surface-to-air missile (SAM) radars that attempted to shoot us down. My four-ship was now about 20 miles behind the mission commander's four-ship and there were six other flights in between. When we were approximately 40 miles south of Baghdad, I saw SAMs searching for the front of the strike package.

SAM launches and break calls filled the radios as the first F-16s bore down on the target. My radar warning receiver (RWR), which is only a rich man's radar detector, beeped and squeaked in my ears that the Iraqi SAM operators were looking at me. Suddenly, I saw a flash off my right wing, then a steady contrail arching upward. At the same time, I heard the call "Magnum" over the radio. Magnum is the Wild Weasel term for launching an antiradiation missile. I smiled to myself, thinking there was one less SAM to worry about. SAMs continued to fill the sky as we approached the target, and the fog of war hit me right between the eyes.

Fifteen miles from the target, I passed two F-16s going the wrong way, completely confusing me and dumping what little situational awareness I thought I had. My immediate reaction was that my flight lead and his wingman had just dropped their bombs and were egressing the target area, almost colliding with me in the process. I immediately queried lead and asked him where he was going since I still showed the target 15 miles in front of me. He quickly responded that he was 13 miles from the target on his bomb run. I said a quick mental prayer thanking the Lord for not letting me screw up. I later learned that the two F-16s that almost hit me had jettisoned their bombs in threat-reacting, and were "getting out of Dodge."

During my bomb run, I was continually dodging SAMs. I committed a fighter's cardinal sin: I lost sight of lead. Under the circumstances there wasn't much I could do. When you are threat-reacting to a SAM, trying to stay alive, you do what needs to be done and worry about the consequences later. Fortunately, my wingman still had me in sight. He was giving us some mutual support as we rolled in on the target. Lead screamed over the radio that the target was obscured by smoke, making it impossible to see. We were dropping dumb bombs, so we didn't have the luxury of laser-guided accuracy. I dropped my bombs where the fire control computer, which was constantly being updated by global positioning system (GPS) satellites, thought the target was. Although not as accurate as laser-guided munitions, that's about as accurate as you can get with dumb bombs, especially on long sorties. I felt the jet "thump" as the bombs released, and I selected full afterburner to get away from the hornet's nest as fast as possible. The RWR continued to howl in my ears, and I could see antiaircraft artillery smoke below me. My fuel was still lower than planned, but not as bad as I had expected. I decided not to jettison my empty fuel tanks yet. I turned for home as fast as the jet would go.

Once I was out of the target area and my RWR quieted, I tried to sort some things out for the RTB. My wingman had lost sight of me while pulling off target, and I was trying to find out where he was. Somehow, he had ended up about 12 miles in front of me. I hooked up with a couple of other F-16s and would worry about my wingman later. He had also found some buddies to race home with. Contrails filled the skies over Iraq as our strike package streaked southward. It reminded me of the movie, *Memphis Belle*. Although I was still over Iraq, about 100 miles north of Saudi, I started to relax. A distressed radio call brought me back to reality. An F-16 had been hit by a SAM and was going down. The pilot was doing his best to keep her flying, keeping his cool on the radio. He pointed south trying to cross the border before his engine let go. He didn't make it. The jet finally quit flying, and he said he was ejecting. Someone said over the strike frequency, like a voice from God, "GOOD LUCK." Later I learned he became one of our first POWs. He was part of a strike package just behind ours, and it hit home like a freight train. At the Saudi border, our four-ship finally re-formed, only to find out that one tanker was to service all 36 jets. I knew a lot of pilots would be scrambling to get there first, and I didn't have time to waste. I told lead I was diverting to the closest Saudi divert field. He said he was headed there too. After landing and shutting down, lead's engine dumped all its oil on the ramp. Maintenance troops told him he probably had less than 5 minutes of flying time left before all the oil was gone, making engine seizure imminent. That was the most serious maintenance problem we had during the war; the jets held up far beyond what we expected.

That completed the most memorable and hair-raising mission I flew in the war. I flew 41 more combat sorties, including going back to Baghdad a week later. None were as threatening as that one. I think psychologists call it a "significant emotional event." It certainly is one I'll never forget, from the takeoff and air refueling, to the harried ingress and high stakes video game of SAM-dodging and threat-reacting. The egress and RTB were forever etched into my mind as I listened to that F-16 pilot trying to nurse his sick airplane home before ejecting. And even though he has returned home safely, I'll never forget the feeling of helplessness as I listened to a brother going down, knowing there wasn't a thing I could do about it.

From Leader to Follower to Leader

by

Capt Bill Iuliano

On 24 January 1991 I flew my first combat mission. It was a strike on a northern Iraqi airfield that culminated six years of training to become mission ready in the F-111 deep-strike role. This is how I had to adapt my role as a leader/follower to the changing environment in wartime.

As an instructor in a fighter squadron, I was an established leader. In the time leading up to Operation Desert Storm, the lieutenant colonels and majors were busy handling the logistics of preparing a squadron for war. Schedules constantly changed, and our leadership busily dealt with the uncertainty of preparing for war. In my view, a big gap opened in how we were going to accomplish our mission—to Fly and Fight! Specifically, were we ready to go to war and put bombs on target?

I was a recent graduate of the USAF Fighter Weapons Instructor Course (FWIC), my fangs were out, and I took the opportunity to train hard within the flying schedule, as did other company grade officers in the squadron who were well trained and just as eager to prepare. It was time to take the lead and fill the gap. A pilot and I decided to run some planning exercises for strikes in Iraq. I called them Iraqi Contingency Ops Planning Exercises or ICOPE. Every Friday we took available aircrews (six to eight people) and gave them a fragmentary order (frag) with a target, time over target (TOT), ordnance, threat arrays, and air assets. They had two hours to plan, and when they finished they briefed the commander with the rest of the squadron watching. Some of these ICOPE exercises were flown locally with other USAFE air assets. The crews eagerly attacked these exercises, and we all felt they were filling the void in our war preparations.

When war finally started, I was left in England awaiting transportation to Incirlik Air Base, Turkey. It took five days, but I finally arrived on 21 January. I was the new guy on the block, and my role shifted to follower as I prepared and flew my first 10 combat missions. The wartime squadron was rank-heavy, with an O-6 and three O-5s, so leadership wasn't a problem. Because of this and the newness of my environment, I decided to follow. Personally speaking, my most rewarding contribution to the war effort came from this shift to follower.

Instead of sawing my fangs off, I redirected my focus to the task at hand—putting bombs on target. Every day, I spent time reviewing radar film of target areas (from my missions and others). I went over every target run with my pilot, and we discussed the accuracy of each attack. Since the accuracy of these attacks depended on where I put the cross hairs, it pressured me into spending extra time studying for the next one. One of the hardest things I did was show my pilot an attack early in the war where I missed the target entirely. I swore to myself I would never miss another target due to lack of preparation. Every mission after that, I looked forward to that final turn toward the target because I was confident in my ability to find it. When I was finally well-settled into my role as follower, I found my name on the next day's schedule as mission commander.

As a mission commander, I was responsible for coordinating an entire package of F-111s and was thrust back into the leadership role. Our mission was a coordinated attack on the oil refineries northwest of Kirkuk in northern Iraq. I put the package together, picked the routes to the target, assigned specific duties to the other flight leads, and briefed the package prior to takeoff. The overall task carried a great deal of responsibility in the 24 hours prior to takeoff.

We took off into a clear, dark night—there was a 40 percent moon illumination. On the ingress, we flew down the Iranian border inside Iraq. The initial point (IP) was a lake with a dam on the end of it. Earlier in the war, we had seen some low AAA around it. As we turned toward the target, I saw a tracer shoot straight up from the dam, like a firework, and burn out about 5,000 feet below us. A second later, a bright flash exploded at our altitude, off the nose. It was followed by two more. I waited for the turbulence, but it never came. The AAA was probably not that close, but my underwear would tell a different story. While we were making our bomb run, I was struggling with a drifting system, using my hands constantly to keep the cursors on the target while still adjusting the radar antenna tilt, contrast, and gains.

My pilot, Maj Tom Poulos, was a 1,500-hour F-111 pilot who flew every mission with me. Our crew coordination was so complete that we talked very little once in enemy territory. On that night, he simply said "look up, Julio," and I glanced up to see the B-52s in our package striking an oil refinery 40 miles off our nose. Five huge columns of fire rose hundreds of feet into the air. It was a sight I'll never forget.

Our bombs came off and impacted the small refinery we had targeted. The target area was still burning when the last jet left Iraq that night. We could see the fires from the Turkish border. The mission was a success, with all targets hit and all aircraft safely home. Long after the war ended, I realized what a huge responsibility my commanders had given me.

As a company grade officer in combat, I had to adapt to each situation presented to me. During Desert Shield, I had to be a leader and get my squadron better prepared for war. When I arrived at Incirlik AB, I had to follow. (I think most company grade officers were followers in war.) Then, when I was put in charge of an entire package, I had to readapt to the leader role and take charge of a strike force of F-111s. No one can deny that the company grade officers were the backbone of the success of Operation Desert Storm. The key to my success was the ability to adapt to the changing environment of war.

A Tanker Navigator's Experience

by

Capt Daniel Nollette

On 11 January 1991, my flight commander ordered me to pack my bags for the desert and show up the next morning ready to fly. I was expecting the call. President Bush had given a deadline, and that deadline was approaching. Still, my wife and I were numb with the realization war would soon be upon us.

All the flight crews received the mission briefing, after which the squadron and wing commanders gave us motivational speeches. (We were the best and they had full confidence in our abilities.) We did not receive any specifics about our mission other than the destination. After the war, we discovered we were replacements for the KC-135s expected to be lost during the first few days of the conflict.

The night the war began, I was sitting in the briefing room. My crew was on "strip alert," which meant we would fly only if a certain mission was implemented. Although I knew the deadline was here, I didn't know exactly when the action would kick off. I knew something had begun when activity in the rooms and hallways increased dramatically.

Information about the war came that night as it did every day and night of the war—via CNN. Bernard Shaw reported that Baghdad was under attack. It had begun!

That night, a sadistic rotational flying cycle began. A typical duty period lasted eight to 12 hours, with flights lasting from four to seven hours. I had from 12 to 16 hours between scheduled duty periods. About once every two weeks I received a 36-hour vacation.

Because the schedule rotated, I flew a day sortie followed by an evening sortie, a night sortie followed by an early morning sortie, and then back around again. I used my free time to eat, sleep, follow the

239

war on CNN, run and work out, and, occasionally, write a letter. Everyone was restricted to the village, a move designed to prevent terrorist incidents. The commander tightened security even more when someone shot at a bus carrying aircrews. After that incident, a Saudi soldier carrying a weapon always rode on the bus.

On one occasion, we joined with four other KC-135s as the number five aircraft. I had never seen a five-ship formation of KC-135s, and all those tankers lined up and spread out below was an impressive sight. But the sight would become even more impressive.

We rendezvoused with several flights of F-16s. As a navigator, my eyes are often in the radarscope or occupied with paperwork, and I was busy at work when the pilot called over interphone, "Hey Nav, check this out!" I moved into the jump seat between the two pilots and looked out the window. The tankers were spread out in a straight line below. Joined up with each tanker was a group of F-16s getting their gas. Off to the sides of each tanker were dozens more F-16s. Like a scene out of a World War II movie, the sky below us, just above the cloud deck, was filled with aircraft.

As we approached the Iraqi border, the first tanker banked 30 degrees left while the rest continued north. Then number two rolled left while his F-16s continued ahead. Numbers three and four followed suit. Finally, we rolled left while our receivers continued north.

Once we were comfortable with the tanker operations, we fell into a pattern. About halfway through the war, someone mentioned there seemed to be a lot of tankers flying at the same altitudes. The operations officer started asking questions, and he discovered that not all the crews were flying their flight plans as they had been briefed. Also, not everyone understood the air tasking order. Tankers were entering and exiting air refueling tracks before they had been scheduled. Tankers flew out to the refueling tracks as planned, but often disregarded planned altitudes on the way home. On several occasions, my pilot noticed a tanker at our altitude flying toward us as we headed out to the area. Many pilots flashed their landing lights if they saw another aircraft at their altitude. The planners soon began to stress the importance of following the flight plan, and there never were any tanker midair collisions.

Despite the tankers' good fortune, not all flyers were spared the hardships of war. The reality of war hit home when the Iraqis displayed captured airmen for the world to see. I had read books about POWs and sat through several code of conduct classes, but I did not absorb the lessons until I saw a fellow aviator, dressed like me, with his face cut and bruised. I felt nauseated and angry. I wanted to drop bombs that day. I wanted to shoot missiles. I wanted to do anything I could to hurt and destroy the enemy. But I resigned myself from such thoughts, knowing my job was worthy in its own right, although the rewards would not be readily observed.

When the Army began moving, I glued myself to CNN. The cease-fire led to a mad scramble to depart. The J-57 engines' elevated noise levels made the KC-135s an unpopular aircraft with the locals, and especially so at a prince's palace below the tanker's departure track. The Saudis were eager to move us out, and we were eager to oblige them. I left as abruptly as I had arrived.

Once Upon a "Mist"y Night...

by

Capt Dave Horton

I will always remember the first night of the air campaign in the Gulf, with its bright flashes of orange and yellow as the first bombs exploded on the horizon like a distant thunderstorm. But I will never forget the second night.

On that night, our KC-135 was the reliability tanker for the F-15 fighter cap near the Iraqi border. Everything went as planned (and practiced) through takeoff. As we passed through 10,000 feet, we entered a cloud deck and the weather simply grew worse as we climbed. At FL 240, Saint Elmo's fire engulfed the windscreen and obscured the nose.

As if this weren't bad enough, we heard the tanker we were replacing report off-station to AWACS. They had orbited for over four hours without a receiver. This was looking like a long, boring night.

After 90 minutes of orbiting in and out of the weather, our crew suddenly jerked back to life as we heard "Mist 24" (an F-117A stealth fighter) calling AWACS for emergency vectors to a divert base for fuel. He asked them to alert the base that he would be arriving on fumes.

Once I heard the AWACS controller's snap vector, I realized we were within 15 miles of his divert flight path. We told AWACS we were available to refuel "Mist 24" if that was better than diverting. After a short discussion, we decided this would be our course of action.

Captain Beer, the copilot, ensured that AWACS closely monitored our rendezvous and cleared our flight paths. A mid-air collision was our biggest concern because of the number of airborne aircraft at 0330L on 18 January. AWACS did this quite well and, after a series

243

of climbs and turns designed to join Mist 24 with us in a clear patch of sky, we watched the air-to-air TACAN click down - 3 DME . . . 2 DME . . . 1 DME . . . 1/2 DME . . . 1 DME . . . 2 DME . . . . Unfortunately, we hadn't yet found that clear patch of sky, and we didn't see each other. The weather was so bad that he couldn't see us although we were lit up like a Christmas tree. The F-117 is hard to see, even on a clear night. We immediately started working another rendezvous with AWACS, and we even tried an ADF holddown. The problem was, every other tanker on the frequency was trying to coach and assist, causing the DF needle to spin wildly.

Our climb finally paid off, and we broke out of the weather intermittently at FL 270. We turned to a heading of 090 degrees when the F-117 reported us in sight at about a mile, in and out of clouds. He had slowed down to his best endurance airspeed to maximize his odds of a successful refueling. Consequently, we had to slow down to 100 knots below his refueling airspeed to give him an airspeed advantage for closure. We dropped flaps to 30 degrees to keep aloft. The problem now was the Iraqi border was only six miles off our nose. Any turns we initiated risked losing Mist 24 in the clouds. Also, as soon as he started a turn, all of his energy would bleed off and he'd probably never catch us. Either situation would negate all of our rendezvous efforts. Taking all this into account, we decided to drive straight ahead, into Iraqi airspace, until we could pass some fuel to Mist 24. That was not an easy decision, since we had no threat-detection capability on the KC-135 other than our friends in the AWACS.

As he closed within 1/2 mile of us, he told us to send our "best boom operator back." He had about 3 minutes of fuel left before he had to "get out of this thing." As such, the boom operator knew he was going to have to use every trick in the book (and then some) to ensure a contact on the first attempt. He didn't tell the F-117 pilot that he was the only boom operator on board.

As it was, Airman Ley didn't see the F-117 until it popped out of the clouds about 100–150 feet in trail, closing quite rapidly. Roughly two minutes after crossing the Iraqi border, we made our initial contact with Mist 24 and pumped him 1,000 pounds of fuel before he was physically pulled from the boom. With the immediate danger out of the way, we began a slooooow turn to the south toward Saudi Arabia. Airman Ley made another contact near the extreme limits of the refueling envelope while I started a toboggan to help the F-117's energy situation and allow him to work more toward the middle of the envelope. The descent took us back down to 15,000 feet and allowed us to accelerate to a proper refueling airspeed. However, it also took us back through the horrendous weather we had worked so hard to climb out of. Airman Ley lost sight of the F-117 on the end of the boom several times, and he said the pilot did an outstanding job just staying on the boom through the clouds, icing, and accompanying turbulence.

The copilot recoordinated with AWACS for a clear route to a known F-117 refueling track. By dropping the F-117 at a known track exit, we felt he could more easily find his way home using ground references if he suffered computer or navigational problems that had precluded rendezvous with his mated tanker. (This was the case as it turned out.) The sun came up by the time we reached the end of the track, and the weather was much more cooperative as we flew from the border.

When he departed for home, Mist 24 was kind enough to thank us and tell the boom, "You really saved my bacon." With that, we told him we were just doing our job and were glad to help.

This was only the second of nearly 40 such jobs we completed during the Gulf War, but one that all tanker crews can take credit for. Anyone in our situation would have done the same thing for a fellow aviator.

The Approach

Refueling

Off and Away

CONTRIBUTORS

Captain Madzuma has a BA from Central Washington University. He is chief, Target Intelligence Branch, 379th Operations Support Squadron, Wurtsmith AFB. He served as chief, Combat Intelligence Branch, 1708th Bombardment Wing (Provisional) at Jedda, Saudi Arabia, during Operation Desert Storm.

Lieutenant Buoniconti has a BA in economics/political science from Yale University. He is the assistant chief, Target Intelligence Branch, Wurtsmith AFB. He was acting chief, Combat Intelligence Branch, 379th Bombardment Wing at Wurtsmith during Operation Desert Storm.

Captain Touhill holds an MS degree from the University of Southern California. He is a three-time winner of the USAF Command, Control, Communications, and Computer Systems Professional Achievement Award, and he is a distinguished graduate of Squadron Officer School. Captain Touhill currently serves as executive officer, 1st Aerospace Communications Group, 55th Wing, Offutt AFB, Nebraska.

Capt John T. Folmar

Lieutenant Brown holds a BS degree from the University of Minnesota Institute of Technology and is a distinguished graduate of ROTC. He led a 20-man Prime BEEF team to first place in the 1990 MAC Readiness Challenge. He is the chief of readiness for the 314th Civil Engineering Squadron at Little Rock AFB, Arkansas.

Captain Grant holds a BBA in management and organization from the University of Miami, Florida. She was commissioned through OTS in December 1989. During the Gulf War, she was chief of personnel utilization, 379th MSSQ. Currently, she is chief of customer assistance at the 8th MSSQ, Kunsan AB, Korea.

Captain Perry holds a bachelor of education media degree from the University of Missouri. After completing OTS, she was operations officer for the 6550th Air Base Group at Patrick AFB, Florida, and food service officer at RAF Alconbury, United Kingdom. Currently, she is force management officer at Charleston AFB, South Carolina.

Captain Marry holds a BA in political science from the US Air Force Academy. He was deployed to Saudi Arabia as security police flight commander from Langley AFB, Virginia. Currently, he is part of the 39th Security Police Flight, Incirlik AB, Turkey.

Captain Fogg holds a master of engineering degree from the University of South Carolina. He is assigned to the 823d RED HORSE Civil Engineering Squadron at Hurlburt Field, Florida. He is now married to the former Miss Margaret Payne of Hilton Head, South Carolina.

Captain Scofidio was commissioned through OTS in 1984. He initially served as a research and development officer at Hanscom AFB, Massachusetts. He was assistant OIC to the 355th "Fighting Falcons" AMU at Myrtle Beach, South Carolina. After deploying, he became OIC of the 353d "Black Panther" AMU.

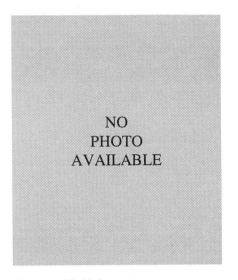

Captain Gatti began his Air Force career as a dental specialist and recruiter. He was a distinguished military graduate of ROTC with a BA in history from Ohio State University. As an honor graduate of the aircraft maintenance officer course, he was assigned to Tyndall AFB, Florida, Taegu AB, ROK, and Hill AFB, Utah. Currently, he is assistant Air National Guard advisor to the Ogden Air Logistics Center commander for Operations/Logistics.

Captain Kieklak

No other name available

Captain Kennedy holds a BS in computer science from the University of Texas at El Paso. He was a distinguished graduate of ROTC. His first assignment was with the 1912 Computer Systems Group at Langley AFB, Virginia. Currently he is the chief of operations, 67 Communications Squadron, Bergstrom AFB, Texas.

Capt Doug Kinneard

Capt Roseanne Warner

Captain Smith has a BS in occupational education. He began his career as a lab technician and academic instructor supervisor. He was both a Titan commander and a GLCM commander. He served as a flight commander at Squadron Officer School. Currently, he is a student at Air Command and Staff College.

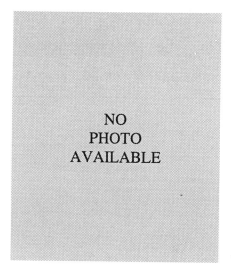

NO
PHOTO
AVAILABLE

Captain Koehler is an instructor navigator with over 1600 hours in the C-130E. He is an honor graduate of Air Combat Command's Air Ground Operations School. During Desert Shield, he served with the 1st Cavalry Division, 1620th Tactical Airlift Squadron (Provisional), and he was the MAC liaison officer to HQ USCENTAF. He participated in the seizure of Rio Hato Airfield during Operation Just Cause. He is currently the tactical airlift liaison officer to the 4th Infantry Division at Fort Carson, Colorado.

Captain Bostrom holds a BS in business administration from John Brown University, Siloam Springs, Arkansas. He enlisted in the Air Force in 1984 and was subsequently trained as a Russian linguist. After completing OTS and UPT, he flew RF-4Cs at Kadena AB, Japan, and Bergstrom AFB, Texas. Currently, he is a T-37 instructor pilot at Columbus AFB, Mississippi.

257

Capt Michael Joy

Captain Scardera holds a BS from the Massachusetts Institute of Technology. He was commissioned through ROTC, but he received an AFIT educational delay to earn an MS in aerospace engineering from the University of Maryland. He worked as an operations crew navigation analyst and a staff navigation analyst at the 2d Satellite Control Squadron. Currently he is an astronautical engineer for the US Space Command Space Control Directorate at Cheyenne Mountain AFB, Colorado. Captain Scardera has written several technical articles related to space operations and exploration.

Captain O'Connell began his career as indications and warning
officer and intelligence operations
officer at 23d Air Division, NORAD,
at Tyndall AFB, Florida. He was
squadron intelligence officer for the
75th Tactical Fighter Squadron and
chief of operational intelligence at
England AFB, Louisiana. He is a
distinguished graduate of the Defense Intelligence College,
Postgraduate Intelligence Program.
Currently, he is assigned to the
Conventional Weapons Effects Division, DIA, at Bolling AFB,
Washington, D.C.

Captain Eanes served as an intelligence applications officer during
Desert Shield/Desert Storm. He
was primarily responsible for evasion and escape issues, but he
also served as acting chief of targets, naval analyst, and OIC of a
combined US/Kuwaiti counterintelli-
gence detachment.

259

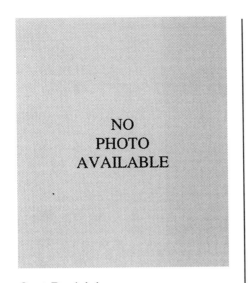

Capt Paul Johnson

Captain Moscarelli holds a master's degree in business administration from Rensselaer Polytechnic Institute, Troy, New York. He is a distinguished graduate of OTS, SOS, and B-52 CCTS. After his initial assignment to the 416th Bombardment Wing at Griffis AFB, New York, he was assigned to Andersen AFB, Guam, and Ellsworth AFB, South Dakota, as a Stan-Eval pilot. Currently, he is assigned to ACSC, Maxwell AFB, Alabama.

NO
PHOTO
AVAILABLE

Lieutenant Clonts has a BA in mechanical engineering from the University of Missouri-Columbia. After ROTC, SUNT, and CCTS, he was assigned to the 596th Bomb Squadron at Barksdale AFB, Louisiana. He is married to the former Cindy Diane Ward of Sacramento, California.

Lieutenant Thagard was a navigator with the 50th TAS at Little Rock AFB, Arkansas, when he deployed to Desert Shield. Currently, he is flying HC-130s at Kadena AB, Okinawa.

Captain Broeking was commissioned through ROTC at Southern Illinois University at Carbondale. He has over 2,500 hours of C-130 time, and he was a standardization and evaluation navigator with the 345th TAS at Yokota AB, Japan, at the time of this story. Currently he is assigned to the 8th Special Operations Squadron at Hurlburt Field, Florida.

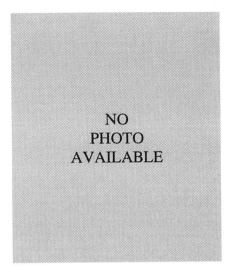

NO PHOTO AVAILABLE

Capt Eric D. Haussermann

Captain Fisher holds an MA in national security studies from California State University, San Bernardino. He has flown F-4Gs at George AFB, California, and Clark AB, Philippines. Currently, he is chief of Current Operations and Training Branch, Northwest Air Defense Sector, McChord AFB, Washington.

Captain O'Grady holds a BS in animal science from Texas A&M. He has flown OA-37s and OA-10s at Osan AB, ROK, and F-16s at Hill AB, Utah. Presently he is assigned to the 366th WG, 389th FS at Mountain Home AFB, Idaho.

Captain Thompson holds a BS in education from the University of Cincinnati. He has over 1,100 hours in the F-16. He has been assigned to Moody AFB, Georgia, and Kunsan AB, ROK. Currently he is an instructor pilot at Eielson AFB, Alaska.

Captain Iuliano is a *magna cum laude* graduate of Daniel Webster College with a BS in computer science. As a distinguished graduate of undergraduate navigator training, he was assigned to F-111s at RAF Upper Heyford in Great Britain. He is a distinguished graduate of the Fighter Weapons Instructor Course. Currently he flies the F-15E with the 4th Fighter Wing at Seymour Johnson AFB, North Carolina.

NO
PHOTO
AVAILABLE

Captain Nollette is an instructor navigator on the KC-135R at Loring AFB, Maine. He received a BS in education from the University of Nebraska-Lincoln and is a graduate of Squadron Officer School. He served as an instructor navigator on the KC-135Q from Beale AFB, California, during Desert Shield/Storm.

Captain Horton holds an astronautical engineering degree from the US Air Force Academy. After he completed undergraduate pilot training, he was assigned to the KC-135 at Grissom AFB, Indiana. He was awarded an air medal for his missions in Desert Storm. He is currently working toward an MS degree in operations research at the Air Force Institute of Technology.

Index